A
MEDITATIVE
COMMENTARY
ON THE
NEW TESTAMENT

MARK: JESUS IS GOD'S SON

A
MEDITATIVE
COMMENTARY
ON THE
NEW TESTAMENT

MARK: JESUS IS GOD'S SON

By Earl Lavender

LEAFWOOD
PUBLISHERS

MARK: JESUS IS GOD'S SON

LEAFWOOD
PUBLISHERS

Copyright 2007 by Earl Lavender

ISBN 978-0-89112-551-8
Printed in the United States of America

Cover design by Greg Jackson, Jackson Design Co., llc

For information contact:
Leafwood Publishers, Abilene, Texas
1-877-816-4455 toll free
www.leafwoodpublishers.com

07 08 09 10 11 12 / 7 6 5 4 3 2 1

To my brother Allen,
God's faithful servant and my faithful friend:
"let us run the race with endurance,
fixing our eyes on Jesus."

ACKNOWLEDGEMENTS

I am deeply thankful to Gary Holloway for partnering with me in this effort. His work in this series is outstanding. I have already used several of his commentaries in various class settings with great response. I am also very thankful to Leonard Allen and Leafwood Publishers. His excitement and support for this effort is a constant encouragement.

A special word of thanks to the Donelson congregation for helping me develop these studies for their use. These brothers and sisters stand as a great example of faith communities committed to the daily study of God's word.

I would also like to offer a special word of thanks to the "early birds" who have for many years so diligently studied the word of God with me every Sunday morning at 7 a.m. If you are ever in Nashville on Sunday, please come and visit. These precious saints will change your life as they have mine.

As always, none of this work could be done without the wonderful and loving support of Rebecca. She has taught me more about the truth of Scripture than anyone else has. Besides Jesus, she is my greatest blessing in this life. I will be forever in her debt for her actively living in God's love as my loving spouse. She is my constant inspiration.

C O N T E N T S

INTRODUCTION:

MEDITATIONS:

INTRODUCTION:

HEARING GOD IN SCRIPTURE

There are many commentaries, guides, and workbooks on the various books of the Bible. How is this series different? It is not intended to answer all your scholarly questions about the Bible, or even make you an expert in the details of Scripture. Instead, this series is designed to help you hear the voice of God in your everyday life. It is a guide to meditation on the Bible, meditation that will allow the Bible to transform you.

We read in many ways. We might scan the newspaper for information, read a map for location, read a novel for pleasure, or read a textbook to pass a test. These are all good ways to read, depending on our circumstances.

A young soldier far away from home who receives a letter from his wife reads in yet another way. He might scan the letter quickly at first for news and information. But his longing for his beloved causes him to read the letter again and again, hearing her sweet voice in every line. He consciously treasures each word of this precious letter.

BIBLE STUDY

So also, there are many good ways to read the Bible, depending on our circumstances. Bible study is absolutely necessary for our life with God. We rightly study the Bible for information. We ask, "Who wrote this?" "When was it written?" "Who were the original readers?"

e words apply to me?" More importantly, we want infor-
God. Who is he? What does he think of me? What does
from me?

There is no substitute for this kind of close, dedicated Bible study.
We must know what the Bible says to know our standing with God.
We therefore read the Bible to discover true doctrine or teaching.
But some—in their emphasis on the authority and inspiration of the
Bible—have forgotten that Bible study is not an end in itself. We want
to know God through Scripture. We want to have a relationship with
the Teacher, not just the teachings.

Jesus tells some of God's people in his day: "You diligently study the
Scriptures because you think that by them you possess eternal life. These
are the Scriptures that testify about me, yet you refuse to come to me to
have life" (John 5:39-40). He's not telling them to study their Bibles less,
but he is reminding them of the deeper purpose of Bible study—to draw
us to God through Jesus. Bible study is a means, not an end.

Yet the way many of us have learned to study the Bible may actually get in the way of hearing God. "Bible study" may sound a lot
like schoolwork, and many of us were happy to get out of school.
"Bible study" may call to mind pictures of intellectuals surrounded
by books in Greek and Hebrew, pondering meanings too deep for
ordinary people. The method of Bible study that has been popular for
some time focuses on the strangeness of the Bible. It was written long
ago, far away, and in languages we cannot read. There is a huge gap
between us and the original readers of the Bible, a gap that can only
be bridged by scholars, not by average folk.

There is some truth and some value in that "scholarly" method. It
is true that the Bible was not written originally to us. Knowing ancient
languages and customs can at times help us understand the Bible
better. However, one unintended result of this approach is to make
the Bible distant from the people of God. We may come to think that
we can only hear God indirectly through Scripture, that his word

must be filtered through scholars. We may even think that deep Bible study is a matter of mastering obscure information about the Bible.

MEDITATION

But we read the Bible for more than information. By studying it, we experience transformation, the mysterious process of God at work in us. Through his loving words, God is calling us to life with him. He is forming us into the image of his Son.

Reading the Bible is not like reading other books. We are not simply trying to learn information or master material. Instead, we want to stand under the authority of Scripture and let God master us. While we read the Bible, it reads us, opening the depths of our being to the overpowering love of God. "For the word of God is living and active. Sharper than any doubleedged sword, it penetrates even to dividing soul and spirit, joints and marrow; it judges the thoughts and attitudes of the heart. Nothing in all creation is hidden from God's sight. Everything is uncovered and laid bare before the eyes of him to whom we must give account" (Hebrews 4:12-13).

Opening our hearts to the word of God is meditation. Although this way of reading the Bible may be new to some, it has a long heritage among God's people. The Psalmist joyously meditates on the words of God (Psalm 1:2; 39:3; 119:15, 23, 27, 48, 78, 97, 99, 148). Meditation is taking the words of Scripture to heart and letting them ask questions of us. It is slowly chewing over a text, listening closely, reading God's message of love to us over and over. This is not a simple, easy, or naïve reading of Scripture, but a process that takes time, dedication, and practice on our part.

There are many ways to meditate on the Bible. One is praying the Scriptures. Prayer and Bible study really cannot be separated. One way of praying the Bible is to make the words of a text your prayer.

Obviously, the prayer texts of Scripture, especially the Psalms, lend themselves to this. "The Lord is my shepherd" has been the prayer of many hearts.

It is proper and helpful to turn the words of the Bible into prayers. Commands from God can become prayers. "You shall have no other gods before me" (Exodus 20:3) can be prayed, "Lord, keep me from anything that takes your place in my heart." Stories can be prayed. Jesus heals a man born blind (John 9), and so we pray, "Lord Jesus open my eyes to who you truly are." Even the promises of the Bible become prayers. "Never will I leave you; never will I forsake you" (Deuteronomy 31:6; Hebrews 13:5) becomes "God help me know that you promise that you are always with me and so live my life without fear."

Obviously, there are many helpful ways of hearing the voice of God in Scripture. Again, the purpose of Bible reading and study is not to know more about the Bible, much less to pride ourselves as experts on Scripture. Instead, we read to hear the voice of our Beloved. We listen for a word from God to us.

Holy Reading

This commentary reflects one ancient way of meditation and praying the Scriptures known as *lectio divina* or holy reading. This method assumes that God wants to speak to us directly in the Bible, that the passage we are reading is God's word to us right now. The writers of the New Testament read the Old Testament with this same conviction. They saw the words of the Bible speaking directly to their own situation. They read with humility and with prayer.

The first step along this way of holy reading is listening to the Bible. Choose a biblical text that is not too long. This commentary breaks Mark into smaller sections. The purpose is to hear God's voice in your current situation, not to cover material or prepare lessons.

Get into a comfortable position and maintain silence before God for several minutes. This prepares the heart to listen. Read slowly. Savor each word. Perhaps read aloud. Listen for a particular phrase that speaks to you. Ask God, "What are you trying to tell me today?"

The next step is to meditate on that particular phrase. That meditation may include slowly repeating the phrase that seems to be for you today. As you think deeply on it, you might even memorize it. Committing biblical passages to memory allows us to hold them in our hearts all day long. If you keep a journal, you might write the passage there. Let those words sink deeply into your heart.

Then pray those words back to God in your heart. Those words may call up visual images, smells, sounds, and feelings. Pay attention to what God is giving you in those words. Then respond in faith to what those words say to your heart. What do they call you to be and to do? Our humble response might take the form of praise, thanksgiving, joy, confession, or even cries of pain.

The final step in this "holy reading" is contemplation of God. The words from God that we receive deeply in our hearts lead us to him. Through these words, we experience union with the all-powerful God of love. And that encounter does not leave us unchanged. Contemplation leads us to kingdom action based on the reading. To what does this reading lead?

What keeps reading the Bible this way from becoming merely our own desires read back into Scripture? How do we know it is God's voice we hear and not our own?

Consider two things. One is prayer. We are asking God to open our hearts, minds, and lives to him. We ask to hear his voice, not ours and not the voice of the world around us.

The second thing that keeps this from being an exercise in self-deception is to study the Bible in community. By praying over Scripture in a group, we hear God's word together. God speaks through the other members of our group. The wisdom he gives them keeps us from private, selfish, and unusual interpretations. They help us keep our own voices in check, as we desire to listen to God alone.

HOW TO USE THIS COMMENTARY

This commentary provides assistance in holy reading of the Bible. It gives structure to daily personal devotions, family meditation, small group Bible studies, and church classes.

DAILY DEVOTIONAL

Listening, meditation, prayer, contemplation—how does this commentary fit into this way of Bible study? Consider it as a conversation partner. We have taken a section of Mark's gospel and broken it down into four short daily readings. After listening, meditating, praying, and contemplating the passage for the day, use the questions suggested in the commentary to provoke deeper reflection. This provides a structure for a daily fifteen minute devotional four days a week. On the fifth day, read the entire passage, meditate, and then use the questions to reflect on the meaning of the whole. On day six, take our meditations on the passage as conversation with another who has prayed over the text.

If you want to begin daily Bible reading but need guidance, this provides a Monday-Saturday experience that prepares the heart for worship and praise on Sunday. This structure also results in a communal reading of Scripture, instead of a private reading. Even if you use this commentary alone, you are not reading privately. God is at work in you and in the conversation you have with another (the author of the commentary) who has sought to hear God through this particular passage of the Bible.

FAMILY BIBLE STUDY

This commentary can also provide an arrangement for family Bible study. Many Christian parents want to lead their children in daily study but don't know where to begin or how to structure their time. Using the six-day plan outlined above means the entire family can read, meditate, pray, and reflect on the shorter passages, using the questions provided. On day five, they can review the entire passage, and then on day six, read the meditations in the commentary to prompt reflection and discussion. God will bless our families beyond our imaginations through the prayerful study of his word.

WEEKLY GROUP STUDY

This commentary can also structure small group Bible study. Each member of the group should have meditated over the daily readings and questions for the five days preceding the group meeting, using the method outlined above. The day before the group meeting, each member should read and reflect on the meditations in the commentary on that passage. You then can meet once a week to hear God's word together. In that group meeting, the method of holy reading would look something like this:

Listening
1. Five minutes of silence.
2. Slow reading of the biblical passage for that week.
3. A minute of silent meditation on the passage.
4. Briefly share with the group the word or phrase that struck you.

Personal Message
5. A second reading of the same passage.
6. A minute of silence.

7. Where does this touch your life today?

8. Responses: I hear, I see, etc.

Life Response

9. Brief silence.

10. What does God want you to do today in light of this text?

Group Prayer

11. Have each member of the group pray aloud for the person on his or her left, asking God to bless the word he has given them.

The procedure suggested here can be used in churches or in neighborhood Bible studies. Church members would use the daily readings Monday-Friday in their daily devotionals. This commentary intentionally provides no readings on the sixth day, so that we can spend Saturdays as a time of rest, not rest from Bible study, but a time to let God's word quietly work its way deep into our hearts. Sunday during Bible school or in home meetings, the group would meet to experience the weekly readings together, using the group method described above. It might be that the sermon for each Sunday could be on the passage for that week.

There are churches that have used this structure to great advantage. Members come to the worship assembly prepared to hear a word from God in that particular text. Much of the background information that is sometimes needed in a sermon has already been given. Preaching can be much more focused on a particular teaching. We strongly urge churches try this type of congregational approach to the study of God's word. In the hallways of those churches who have embraced this type of study, the talk is not of the local football team or the weather, but of the shared experience of the Word of God for that week.

And that is the purpose of our personal and communal study, to hear the voice of God, our loving Father who wants us to love him in return. He deeply desires a personal relationship with us. Father, Son, and Spirit make a home inside us (see John 14:16-17, 23). Our loving God speaks to his children! But we must listen for his voice. That listening is not a matter of gritting our teeth and trying harder to hear. Instead, it is part of our entire life with God. That is what Bible study is all about.

Through daily personal prayer and meditation on God's word, and through a communal reading of Scripture, our most important conversation partner—the Holy Spirit—will do his mysterious and marvelous work. Among other things, the Spirit pours God's love into our hearts (Romans 5:5), bears witness to our spirits that we are God's children (Romans 8:16), intercedes for us with God (Romans 8:26), and enlightens us as to God's will (Ephesians 1:17).

So this is an invitation to personal daily Bible study, to praying the Scriptures, to sharing with fellow believers, to hearing the voice of God. God will bless us, our families, our churches, and his world if we take the time to be still, listen, and be obedience to his word.

THE SPIRITUALITY OF THE GOSPEL ACCORDING TO MARK

Mark wastes no time identifying the purpose of his account of the gospel. It is to tell the good news of Jesus Christ, the Son of God. Mark's account is fast moving and succinct. He includes little discourse material, choosing instead to focus on Jesus' actions. At times, it seems he is in a hurry to tell the story. There is an unmistakable urgency to his message. There was a great need for the story and teachings of Jesus to be carefully passed on (the eyewitnesses were aging and dying). There was also a crucial need for the good news to be told in such a way that it sustained believers struggling with persecution. To that end, Mark's gospel takes the reader beyond a simplistic triumphalism (if I am good to God, he will give me an easy and happy life) by framing the story of Jesus in a context of radical servanthood and suffering. Ultimately, for the believer in Jesus, there will be victory and glory (at the coming of the Son of Man—Mark 13), but in the meantime being a true follower calls for patient suffering and perhaps even physical death.

The spirituality of Mark's gospel focuses on two interrelated themes—the true nature of the reign (or kingdom) of God and authentic discipleship. In coming to understand the purpose and function of the reign of God on the earth, one willingly embraces the full commitment necessary to be an authentic apprentice of Jesus, the Son of God.

The Kingdom Of God

The first words of Jesus in Mark's gospel are: "The time has come. The kingdom of God is near. Repent and believe the good news!" (1:15). What is the kingdom and why does it require a total reorientation of life (repentance) in order to embrace it? These are major questions addressed throughout Mark. The transcendent God has drawn near to humankind through the person and work of Jesus Christ, his Son. God lovingly invites into his dynamic reign those willing to turn away from this world and accept new eyes, ears, and hearts.

But the journey into God's kingdom is a difficult and challenging one. The only gate into the kingdom is following Jesus Christ into the radical life of living as children of God. Jesus, the Son of God, invites us into authentic discipleship through his life and teachings.

AUTHENTIC DISCIPLESHIP

A wonderful description of salvation life is receiving by God's grace the eyes, ears, and hands of Jesus through the transformation of the Holy Spirit. We would then see, hear, and do what Jesus would do if he were in our bodies with our abilities and gifts. This is the key to abundant life—allowing Jesus to live in us. The tension in the gospel of Mark is between those who understood the meaning of discipleship and those who were not able to see or hear what Jesus was offering. In a sense, the tension was between authentic and inauthentic spirituality. Those manifesting an inauthentic spirituality did not see and hear what Jesus taught concerning the kingdom of God. This involved two important groups. The first comes as no surprise. It was comprised of the religious leaders who opposed Jesus from the beginning to the end of his ministry. For them, Jesus represented a threat to their positions of power and their basic view of life in God. The second group shocks us—it was Jesus' own disciples. Though they walked with him, they did not understand the meaning of what he did and taught. Their minds were so fixed on what they wanted, they could not see what God was offering through Christ. Both groups were trying to be religious, but their efforts led them to oppose Jesus rather than follow him.

Mark challenges the reader to move beyond the comfortable life of religious behavior into the uncertainty of radical discipleship, to become a true member of Jesus' family (Mark 3:31-34). This happens when one fully submits to the will of God. And who better could identify this life than the faithful Son of God?

Our challenge as we read and meditate on this text, is to ask where we are in Mark's account of the life of Jesus. Will we accept him as the Son of God? Will we accept what he says is true about our lives? Will we be authentic disciples? Will we tell others of what we have seen and heard? Will we become a part of what Jesus is doing in our world?

LONG ENDING OR SHORT?

Most translations of Mark's gospel note that the most reliable and early manuscripts as well as other ancient witnesses do not include verses 9-20 of chapter sixteen. While it is not the purpose of this meditative commentary to offer technical information about manuscripts, whether Mark ended his account of the story of Jesus with the short or long ending does impact its message.

Many scholars are convinced that verses 9-20 were added some time after the completion of Mark. Some believe the book should actually end with verse 8, others suggest it would be odd to end a book with women full of fear, not following the directions of the white robed young man (an angel?) to go and tell of the resurrection.

This commentary offers a meditation on the longer ending because so many have been spiritually strengthened by these verses. Even if they were added later (as I am inclined to believe), they seem to be an assimilation of other post-resurrection materials. The content of these verses is affirmed by other passages of Scripture.

The abrupt ending of verse 8 offers an intriguing possibility. Mark calls us to believe in Jesus as the Son of God. The text leaves no doubt about the resurrection. In chapter sixteen, the stone was rolled away; the tomb was empty. The young man in white robes (surely an angel) announced the resurrection of Jesus the Nazarene. Now, what will you, the reader, do with this fact? It may seem bewildering, but reflect back on all that Jesus said about his death, burial, and resurrection throughout the text of Mark. What will you now do? I believe Mark wants us to say, "Jesus is indeed God's Son, and he is risen!"

THE BEGINNING OF THE GOOD NEWS
(1:1-20)

DAY ONE READING AND QUESTIONS

¹:¹The beginning of the gospel about Jesus Christ, the Son of God.
²It is written in Isaiah the prophet:

"I will send my messenger ahead of you,

who will prepare your way"

³"a voice of one calling in the desert,

'Prepare the way for the Lord,

make straight paths for him.' "

⁴And so John came, baptizing in the desert region and preaching a baptism of repentance for the forgiveness of sins. ⁵The whole Judean countryside and all the people of Jerusalem went out to him. Confessing their sins, they were baptized by him in the Jordan River. ⁶John wore clothing made of camel's hair, with a leather belt around his waist, and he ate locusts and wild honey. ⁷And this was his message: "After me will come one more powerful than I, the thongs of whose sandals I am not worthy to stoop down and untie. ⁸ I baptize you with water, but he will baptize you with the Holy Spirit."

1. *How would you summarize the content of "the gospel about Jesus Christ, the Son of God?" Why is this good news?*

2. *Why do you think so many people went out to the desert to hear the message of John?*

3. How do you think John's ministry would be accepted in today's church? Why?

DAY TWO READING AND QUESTIONS

⁹At that time Jesus came from Nazareth in Galilee and was baptized by John in the Jordan. ¹⁰As Jesus was coming up out of the water, he saw heaven being torn open and the Spirit descending on him like a dove. ¹¹And a voice came from heaven: "You are my Son, whom I love; with you I am well pleased."

¹²At once the Spirit sent him out into the desert, ¹³and he was in the desert forty days, being tempted by Satan. He was with the wild animals, and angels attended him.

1. Why do you think Jesus was baptized? How does this affect you as his disciple?

2. What is so important about the message from the heavenly voice?

3. Why do you think the Spirit immediately led Jesus into a time of trial and temptation?

DAY THREE READING AND QUESITONS

¹⁴After John was put in prison, Jesus went into Galilee, proclaiming the good news of God. ¹⁵"The time has come," he said. "The kingdom of God is near. Repent and believe the good news!"

1. What is "the good news of God?"

2. What is "the kingdom of God?"

3. Why is it necessary to repent in order to embrace the good news?

DAY FOUR READING AND QUESTIONS

[16]As Jesus walked beside the Sea of Galilee, he saw Simon and his brother Andrew casting a net into the lake, for they were fishermen. [17]"Come, follow me," Jesus said, "and I will make you fishers of men." [18]At once they left their nets and followed him.

[19]When he had gone a little farther, he saw James son of Zebedee and his brother John in a boat, preparing their nets. [20]Without delay he called them, and they left their father Zebedee in the boat with the hired men and followed him.

1. *Why do think Simon and Andrew, James and John were willing to follow Jesus?*

2. *What were they willing to leave behind?*

3. *Do you consider yourself an active disciple of Jesus? Why or why not?*

DAY FIVE READING AND QUESTIONS

Reread the entire text (1:1-20).

1. *Do you actively and easily share the good news of Jesus the Messiah? Why or why not?*

2. *Recall the moment of your baptism. Do you feel God's affirmation that you are his beloved child? Why or why not?*

3. *Have you heard Jesus' call to repent and believe the good news? Why or why not?*

MEDITATION

Mark wastes little time with details. His account is one of fast moving action. His brief introduction of the ministry of Jesus is almost too abrupt. In the first twenty verses of Mark's account, John's ministry is explained, Jesus' baptism occurs, the temptations are quickly accounted for, and the first disciples are called. The story moves at a fast pace.

One of our challenges in this study is to slow the story down a bit and carefully digest this amazing account. This is the gospel, the good news, about Jesus Christ, the Son of God. It is the telling of God's wonderful act of redemption, in which he broke into history in the person of his Son. This is it—the gospel! So, are we willing to follow John out to the wilderness (out of the comfort of our self-focused lives) and hear his call for repentance? Will we confess our wrongful living and embrace God's call to radically reorient our lives in the context of his rule? Do our hearts beat fast as we hear of one who will immerse us with God's Holy Spirit?

And then Jesus appears. He calls us to follow him to new life, an existence fully submitted to God. After his baptism, God's voice affirms what we hold dear—Jesus is the beloved Son of God! We want to stop and enjoy this wonderful moment of affirmation, but the story quickly moves to forty days of trial. The Son is faithful throughout and God sends his angels to attend to his needs.

Now Jesus speaks for the first time in Mark's account. "The time has come—the kingdom of God is near. Repent and believe the good news." Indeed, the time has come. Jesus immediately calls his first disciples. It is here that we enter the gospel story. Will we repent and believe? Will we follow? Will we listen to his words? Will we leave our comfortable world and become those who work to gather and reclaim God's children for him from the seas of life?

The urgency of the story is not that Mark lacked time or paper. Jesus Christ is risen. There is a story to tell. But until we walk with Jesus and understand his call, the good news of the kingdom is yet unlearned. May we have eyes to see, ears to hear, and hearts ready to be broken.

"Dear Jesus Christ, the Son of God, open my heart to the gospel that I may walk in your ways, bearing witness to the kingdom of God."

THE POWER OF THE KINGDOM
(1:21-45)

DAY ONE READING AND QUESTIONS

²¹They went to Capernaum, and when the Sabbath came, Jesus went into the synagogue and began to teach. ²²The people were amazed at his teaching, because he taught them as one who had authority, not as the teachers of the law. ²³Just then a man in their synagogue who was possessed by an evil spirit cried out, ²⁴"What do you want with us, Jesus of Nazareth? Have you come to destroy us? I know who you are—the Holy One of God!"

²⁵"Be quiet!" said Jesus sternly. "Come out of him!" ²⁶The evil spirit shook the man violently and came out of him with a shriek.

²⁷The people were all so amazed that they asked each other, "What is this? A new teaching—and with authority! He even gives orders to evil spirits and they obey him." ²⁸News about him spread quickly over the whole region of Galilee.

1. What do Jesus' actions on the Sabbath tell us about the Sabbath?

2. What do you think caused people to attribute authority to what Jesus taught? What made his teaching stand out when compared to the teachers of the law?

3. Why would Jesus not allow the evil spirit to identify him as the "Holy One of God"?

DAY TWO READING AND QUESTIONS

²⁹As soon as they left the synagogue, they went with James and John to the home of Simon and Andrew. ³⁰Simon's mother-in-law was in bed with a fever, and they told Jesus about her. ³¹So he went to her, took her hand and helped her up. The fever left her and she began to wait on them.

³²That evening after sunset the people brought to Jesus all the sick and demon-possessed. ³³The whole town gathered at the door, ³⁴and Jesus healed many who had various diseases. He also drove out many demons, but he would not let the demons speak because they knew who he was.

1. Why do you think the healing of Simon's mother-in-law is included in this account?

2. How does Jesus' healing of so many influence your view of Jesus?

3. Why would the demons know who Jesus was?

DAY THREE READING AND QUESTIONS

³⁵Very early in the morning, while it was still dark, Jesus got up, left the house and went off to a solitary place, where he prayed. ³⁶Simon and his companions went to look for him, ³⁷and when they found him, they exclaimed: "Everyone is looking for you!"

³⁸Jesus replied, "Let us go somewhere else—to the nearby villages—so I can preach there also. That is why I have come." ³⁹So he traveled throughout Galilee, preaching in their synagogues and driving out demons.

1. Once again, we are told of a behavior of Jesus that is helpful in our understanding of him. What did he do in this account that he did often—likely many times a day?

2. Why was everyone looking for Jesus?

3. Why did Jesus decide to move on from Capernaum?

DAY FOUR READING AND QUESTIONS

[40]A man with leprosy came to him and begged him on his knees, "If you are willing, you can make me clean."

[41]Filled with compassion, Jesus reached out his hand and touched the man. "I am willing," he said. "Be clean!" [42] Immediately the leprosy left him and he was cured.

[43]Jesus sent him away at once with a strong warning: [44]"See that you don't tell this to anyone. But go, show yourself to the priest and offer the sacrifices that Moses commanded for your cleansing, as a testimony to them." [45]Instead he went out and began to talk freely, spreading the news. As a result, Jesus could no longer enter a town openly but stayed outside in lonely places. Yet the people still came to him from everywhere.

1. What do we know of the leper's faith?

2. Why would Jesus' touching the man be unusual?

3. Why do you think Jesus warned the leper not to tell what Jesus had done?

DAY FIVE READING AND QUESTIONS

Reread the entire passage (1:21-45).

1. What does Jesus do from the very beginning of his ministry? What does this tell us about what we ought to be doing?

2. How might we teach the good news of Jesus in a way that those listening would attribute authority to our words?

3. What does Jesus' practice of prayer call us to do? When is it appropriate for us to pray?

MEDITATION

Because of the brevity and fast pace of Mark's gospel, it is important to pay close attention to specific behaviors of Jesus. Note how Jesus organized his life. It calls us to question how we arrange ours. Jesus was a teacher. He used every opportunity in his life to proclaim the good news of the kingdom of God. On Sabbaths he would head to the synagogue and teach. On other days he would walk with his disciples and teach. And his teaching grabbed attention. When he spoke, people were stunned at the authority with which he spoke. How does "authority" manifest itself? You might say, "Well, of course, Jesus performed powerful miracles that clearly manifested his authority." But note that the people were astonished with his teaching *before* he performed miracles. Something about his teaching itself amazed his listeners.

Authority is evident when one is speaking truth with embodied conviction. Jesus lived what he taught, so he could speak of the kingdom of God with convincing authority. His teaching was an expression of who he was. It is not by chance that the first miracle of Jesus in Mark is the casting out of an evil spirit. Satan was intent on destroying Jesus' work of proclaiming God's kingdom. The confrontation was brief—the power of Satan was no match for the power of the Son of God. And Satan, through his demons, was not allowed to identify Jesus for who he was. The honor of proclaiming Jesus as God's Son would be given to those who declared it in convicted faith.

Now that Jesus' kingdom announcement had begun, he healed many and cast out countless demons. His fame grew rapidly. Even though the sun was down (imagine complete darkness—a time when few would risk traveling), the sick and demon possessed were brought to him. So what did Jesus do with all this newfound popularity? Early the next morning, he went out to a deserted place and prayed. Have you ever done this? What a wonderful discipline! When good things happen, affirm them alone before God. Seek direction. Jesus' ministry was not one primarily of healing. While these compassionate acts were marvelous testimony to his power and love, his work was to proclaim the message of God's kingdom to all the surrounding towns.

Consider for a moment the healing of the leper. Can you imagine what it must have been like to feel the touch of Jesus? It had been so long since that man had experienced anything but disgust from a nonleper. Jesus was not only willing to heal him, but to compassionately touch him.

Teach with authority. Act with kindness and compassion. Touch the outcast. Find a quiet place to seek direction in your life—daily. There is so much to learn from Jesus.

"Dear Lord, keep me focused on your plan for my life. Help me to see the teaching opportunities that you provide. May I faithfully experience kingdom life in such a way that I can speak of it with authority when the opportunities present themselves."

THE CONFLICT BEGINS

(2:1-3:6)

DAY ONE READING AND QUESTIONS

[1]A few days later, when Jesus again entered Capernaum, the people heard that he had come home. [2]So many gathered that there was no room left, not even outside the door, and he preached the word to them. [3]Some men came, bringing to him a paralytic, carried by four of them. [4]Since they could not get him to Jesus because of the crowd, they made an opening in the roof above Jesus and, after digging through it, lowered the mat the paralyzed man was lying on. [5]When Jesus saw their faith, he said to the paralytic, "Son, your sins are forgiven."

[6]Now some teachers of the law were sitting there, thinking to themselves, [7]"Why does this fellow talk like that? He's blaspheming! Who can forgive sins but God alone?"

[8]Immediately Jesus knew in his spirit that this was what they were thinking in their hearts, and he said to them, "Why are you thinking these things? [9]Which is easier: to say to the paralytic, 'Your sins are forgiven,' or to say, 'Get up, take your mat and walk'? [10]But that you may know that the Son of Man has authority on earth to forgive sins...." He said to the paralytic, [11]"I tell you, get up, take your mat and go home." [12]He got up, took his mat and walked out in full view of them all. This amazed everyone and they praised God, saying, "We have never seen anything like this!"

1. Why were the friends of the paralytic so desperate to get him to Jesus?

2. What was Jesus' response to the teachers who were thinking he was guilty of blasphemy?

3. Stop for a moment and try to visualize what the crowds around Jesus saw and how they must have reacted when the atrophied, paralyzed man stood and picked up his bed. Can you imagine the joyful surprise and excited praise?

DAY TWO READING AND QUESTIONS

[13]Once again Jesus went out beside the lake. A large crowd came to him, and he began to teach them. [14]As he walked along, he saw Levi son of Alphaeus sitting at the tax collector's booth. "Follow me," Jesus told him, and Levi got up and followed him.

[15]While Jesus was having dinner at Levi's house, many tax collectors and "sinners" were eating with him and his disciples, for there were many who followed him. [16]When the teachers of the law who were Pharisees saw him eating with the "sinners" and tax collectors, they asked his disciples: "Why does he eat with tax collectors and 'sinners'?"

[17]On hearing this, Jesus said to them, "It is not the healthy who need a doctor, but the sick. I have not come to call the righteous, but sinners."

1. What do you think Jesus taught most often to those who were listening?

2. Why is it unusual that Jesus would call Levi to follow him?

3. Are you surprised that Jesus kept company with "sinners" and tax collectors? To what would this be similar in our culture?

DAY THREE READING AND QUESTIONS

[18]Now John's disciples and the Pharisees were fasting. Some people came and asked Jesus, "How is it that John's disciples and the disciples of the Pharisees are fasting, but yours are not?"

[19]Jesus answered, "How can the guests of the bridegroom fast while he is with them? They cannot, so long as they have him with them. [20]But the time will come when the bridegroom will be taken from them, and on that day they will fast.

[21]"No one sews a patch of unshrunk cloth on an old garment. If he does, the new piece will pull away from the old, making the tear worse. [22]And no one pours new wine into old wineskins. If he does, the wine will burst the skins, and both the wine and the wineskins will be ruined. No, he pours new wine into new wineskins."

1. *Why would anyone be concerned that the disciples of Jesus were not fasting?*

2. *Did Jesus say his disciples would ever fast? When? Does this call us to fast?*

3. *What do you think Jesus was comparing to "patching materials" (that is, what is "the patch" and what is the "old wineskin")? Why were these incompatible?*

DAY FOUR READING AND QUESTIONS

[23]One Sabbath Jesus was going through the grainfields, and as his disciples walked along, they began to pick some heads of grain. [24]The Pharisees said to him, "Look, why are they doing what is unlawful on the Sabbath?"

[25]He answered, "Have you never read what David did when he and his companions were hungry and in need? [26] In the days of Abiathar the high priest, he entered the house of God and ate the consecrated bread, which is lawful only for priests to eat. And he also gave some to his companions."

[27]Then he said to them, "The Sabbath was made for man, not man for the Sabbath. [28]So the Son of Man is Lord even of the Sabbath."

^{3:1}Another time he went into the synagogue, and a man with a shriveled hand was there. ²Some of them were looking for a reason to accuse Jesus, so they watched him closely to see if he would heal him on the Sabbath. ³Jesus said to the man with the shriveled hand, "Stand up in front of everyone."

⁴Then Jesus asked them, "Which is lawful on the Sabbath: to do good or to do evil, to save life or to kill?" But they remained silent.

⁵He looked around at them in anger and, deeply distressed at their stubborn hearts, said to the man, "Stretch out your hand." He stretched it out, and his hand was completely restored. ⁶Then the Pharisees went out and began to plot with the Herodians how they might kill Jesus.

1. *What did those observing the disciples deem as unlawful? Why?*

2. *What was Jesus teaching about God by using this particular story involving David?*

3. *Why were the religious leaders so concerned about the sabbath? How were they missing the point?*

DAY FIVE READING AND QUESTIONS

Reread the entire text (2:1-3:6).

1. *How might we be so attractive to the hurting and broken in our world that they would take risks to appear before us for help?*

2. *Should we be involved in fasting? Why or why not?*

3. *What are some issues we might use to pass improper judgment on others as did the Pharisees?*

MEDITATION

What amazing events! There is so much to consider in just this chapter's portrayal of Jesus. The story of the healed paralytic is too wonderful for words! We see deep friendship—an authentic and committed love. The paralytic must have been someone special to have such friends. They were so desperate to get their friend in front of Jesus they were willing to vandalize a home in order to let the man through the roof to Jesus. Where would you be in this story? Among the crowd blocking the way to Jesus, inhibiting those who desperately needed him from getting close? Would you be the hopeless one on the mat in need of healing? The friends who risked all to help? The Pharisees who sneered at what they saw as presumptuous behavior on the part of Jesus? Or would you be Jesus? Are you the kind of person the hurting seek out for healing? Do the friends of those needing healing seek you out?

I have been all of these. Too seldom I have been Jesus in this story. I find myself too wrapped up in my own self-centeredness. I forget that followers of Jesus have the power through the work of God to heal those paralyzed by sin. Jesus' granting of forgiveness was a greater gift than physical healing. We continue that ministry of ultimate healing as we share the word of life with those around us.

It is not by chance that we move from this magnificent miracle to Jesus calling Levi. Jesus confronted another person paralyzed by sin and lovingly invited Levi to follow him into kingdom life. Then Jesus did something that surprises us. He accepted Levi's invitation to come to a party for his friends. The only friends a tax collector had were other known sinners. Most regarded tax collectors as extorters and cheats (because most were), so their only friends were others who intentionally lived in sin. And Jesus just walked right into the middle of them and sat at their table! How could one we believe to be the embodiment of holiness associate with such people? Here is the irony—one who is holy (set apart for God's purposes) should find himself among such people. For how else will sinful people hear the good news and repent? "Holy" does not mean we stay away from sinners; it means we are set apart to be God's agents of redemption anywhere people are seeking life.

Jesus' new, authoritative teaching and way of life just did not fit the expectations of the religious leaders. The behavior of his disciples further discredited Jesus. They did not fast, they dared work on the Sabbath (rolling the heads of wheat in their hands to eat the kernels constituted work for the Pharisees!)—how could their leader be a teacher of truth?

These religious "rule-keepers" even exploited those suffering to see if Jesus himself would break their rules of Sabbath behavior. They had no concern for the tragic circumstance of the man with the withered hand. They used him to test Jesus. And Jesus failed their test of "righteous" behavior. He dared to heal, even on the Sabbath. What better use of God's day of rest than to restore life to the hurting?

Jesus explained that authentic kingdom life simply would not fit into the religious system created by these men. New containers were needed—no patching onto the old would do. No, Jesus had come to introduce a loving God who desperately wanted his people to find life—true life. This is the rest that all humankind still seeks. Rigid systems of religious behavior cannot contain the dynamic life of God's kingdom. In fact, they work against it. The Lord of the Sabbath has come. Get ready to be stretched!

"Lord of the Sabbath, help me find true rest in you. Heal my paralyzed heart, open my eyes and ears. Help me see the life to which I have been called in God's kingdom."

JESUS CHOOSES THE TWELVE

(3:7-35)

DAY ONE READING AND QUESTIONS

⁷Jesus withdrew with his disciples to the lake, and a large crowd from Galilee followed. ⁸When they heard all he was doing, many people came to him from Judea, Jerusalem, Idumea, and the regions across the Jordan and around Tyre and Sidon. ⁹Because of the crowd he told his disciples to have a small boat ready for him, to keep the people from crowding him. ¹⁰For he had healed many, so that those with diseases were pushing forward to touch him. ¹¹Whenever the evil spirits saw him, they fell down before him and cried out, "You are the Son of God." ¹²But he gave them strict orders not to tell who he was.

1. Why do you think Jesus withdrew from the crowds so often?

2. What about Jesus attracted the crowds?

3. Why do you think the demons repeatedly acknowledged the true identity of Jesus?

DAY TWO READING AND QUESTIONS

¹³Jesus went up on a mountainside and called to him those he wanted, and they came to him. ¹⁴He appointed twelve—designating them apostles—that they might be with him and that he might send

them out to preach [15]and to have authority to drive out demons. [16]These are the twelve he appointed: Simon (to whom he gave the name Peter); [17]James son of Zebedee and his brother John (to them he gave the name Boanerges, which means Sons of Thunder); [18]Andrew, Philip, Bartholomew, Matthew, Thomas, James son of Alphaeus, Thaddaeus, Simon the Zealot [19]and Judas Iscariot, who betrayed him.

1. For what purose did Jesus appoint the twelve?

2. What authority did Jesus give them?

3. Why would twelve, as a number, have a special significance to the Jews?

DAY THREE READING AND QUESTIONS

[20]Then Jesus entered a house, and again a crowd gathered, so that he and his disciples were not even able to eat. [21]When his family heard about this, they went to take charge of him, for they said, "He is out of his mind."

[22]And the teachers of the law who came down from Jerusalem said, "He is possessed by Beelzebub! By the prince of demons he is driving out demons."

[23]So Jesus called them and spoke to them in parables: "How can Satan drive out Satan? [24]If a kingdom is divided against itself, that kingdom cannot stand. [25]If a house is divided against itself, that house cannot stand. [26]And if Satan opposes himself and is divided, he cannot stand; his end has come. [27]In fact, no one can enter a strong man's house and carry off his possessions unless he first ties up the strong man. Then he can rob his house. [28]I tell you the truth, all the sins and blasphemies of men will be forgiven them. [29]But whoever blasphemes against the Holy Spirit will never be forgiven; he is guilty of an eternal sin."

[30]He said this because they were saying, "He has an evil spirit."

1. *What concerning Jesus' behavior troubled his family?*

2. *What do you think Jesus' family was going to do with him?*

3. *What specific words of those opposing Jesus caused him to warn of an unforgivable sin?*

DAY FOUR READING AND QUESTIONS

[31]Then Jesus' mother and brothers arrived. Standing outside, they sent someone in to call him. [32]A crowd was sitting around him, and they told him, "Your mother and brothers are outside looking for you."

[33]"Who are my mother and my brothers?" he asked.

[34]Then he looked at those seated in a circle around him and said, "Here are my mother and my brothers! [35]Whoever does God's will is my brother and sister and mother."

1. *Why do you think Jesus' family sent someone in to tell him they had arrived?*

2. *What was Jesus saying about true family with his words?*

3. *What does Jesus' comment about family say to us?*

DAY FIVE READING AND QUESTIONS

Reread the entire text (3:7-35).

1. *Do you take the time for personal spiritual retreats? Consider setting a day apart for time alone with God.*

2. *Now that the twelve apostles have been identified as those chosen to preach and cast out demons, what do you expect of them as the story of Jesus' ministry continues? (Pretend you do not know the rest of the story.)*

3. *Is it possible for us to attribute to Satan that which God has done because of our misplaced religious convictions? How can we keep from doing this?*

4. *Do you think of yourself as a brother or sister of Jesus? Why or why not?*

MEDITATION

Once again we find Mark pointing out that Jesus withdrew from the crowds for time alone with God. Because of Jesus' popularity, this was not an easy task. Nonetheless, Jesus did this regularly. If Jesus the Son of God needed time alone with God, how much more do we? It was in such a setting that Jesus appointed "the twelve." What a joy that must have been—to be chosen by Jesus to participate in his work of defeating evil! Is our call to authentic discipleship any less significant?

Can you imagine how Jesus must have felt, surrounded constantly by those wanting his attention? Some sought healing, others a blessing, and some just wanted to hear his words. It came to the point he could not even eat—which rightfully worried his family. Even those closest to Jesus did not understand his giving heart. His unusual behavior (total giving of self for those he could serve) led some to suggest he was "possessed" by the devil himself.

Jesus pointed out the fallacy of such thinking. Satan would not cast out himself. Jesus' actions demonstrated, not compliance with Satan, but authority over him. Here we see the danger of religious systems that limit the work of God. Because a person's behavior is less than we expect, we feel justified in condemning the activity and the person. But in so doing, we may be working directly against the Holy Spirit. That is exactly what the teachers of the law were doing. Attributing God's work to Satan because of their unwillingness to repent, they found themselves outside hope of God's reconciling grace.

Mark concludes this episode with Jesus' family arriving to rescue him from his "crazy behavior." When told that his family sought him, Jesus identified his true family. Through the centuries of Christian history, his words ring out to reassure those of us who seek to follow him: "Here are my mother and my brothers! Whoever does God's will is my brother and sister and mother."

"Dearest brother, how can we thank you for what you have done for us? You have invited us into intimate relationship with your Father. Please give us more of your inexhaustible love for the hurting, that we may truly do the will of God in our lives."

PARABLES ABOUT THE KINGDOM
(4:1-34)

DAY ONE READING AND QUESTIONS

[1]Again Jesus began to teach by the lake. The crowd that gathered around him was so large that he got into a boat and sat in it out on the lake, while all the people were along the shore at the water's edge. [2]He taught them many things by parables, and in his teaching said: [3]"Listen! A farmer went out to sow his seed. [4]As he was scattering the seed, some fell along the path, and the birds came and ate it up. [5]Some fell on rocky places, where it did not have much soil. It sprang up quickly, because the soil was shallow. [6]But when the sun came up, the plants were scorched, and they withered because they had no root. [7]Other seed fell among thorns, which grew up and choked the plants, so that they did not bear grain. [8]Still other seed fell on good soil. It came up, grew and produced a crop, multiplying thirty, sixty, or even a hundred times."

[9]Then Jesus said, "He who has ears to hear, let him hear."

1. *Why do you think Jesus used parables in his teaching?*

2. *How do you think the crowds reacted to Jesus teaching with parables or stories?*

3. *Do you enjoy meditating on the parables of Jesus? Why or why not?*

DAY TWO READING AND QUESTIONS

[10]When he was alone, the Twelve and the others around him asked him about the parables. [11]He told them, "The secret of the kingdom of God has been given to you. But to those on the outside everything is said in parables [12]so that,

" 'they may be ever seeing but never perceiving,
and ever hearing but never understanding;
otherwise they might turn and be forgiven!'"

[13]Then Jesus said to them, "Don't you understand this parable? How then will you understand any parable? [14]The farmer sows the word. [15]Some people are like seed along the path, where the word is sown. As soon as they hear it, Satan comes and takes away the word that was sown in them. [16]Others, like seed sown on rocky places, hear the word and at once receive it with joy. [17]But since they have no root, they last only a short time. When trouble or persecution comes because of the word, they quickly fall away. [18]Still others, like seed sown among thorns, hear the word; [19]but the worries of this life, the deceitfulness of wealth and the desires for other things come in and choke the word, making it unfruitful. [20]Others, like seed sown on good soil, hear the word, accept it, and produce a crop—thirty, sixty or even a hundred times what was sown."

1. Why do you think Jesus told the disciples about "the secret of the kingdom"?

2. Why would Jesus hide the message of the kingdom from some of his listeners?

3. Which of the described soils are most like the "soil" of your heart? Why?

DAY THREE READING AND QUESTIONS

²¹He said to them, "Do you bring in a lamp to put it under a bowl or a bed? Instead, don't you put it on its stand? ²²For whatever is hidden is meant to be disclosed, and whatever is concealed is meant to be brought out into the open. ²³If anyone has ears to hear, let him hear."

²⁴"Consider carefully what you hear," he continued. "With the measure you use, it will be measured to you—and even more. ²⁵Whoever has will be given more; whoever does not have, even what he has will be taken from him."

1. What do you think Jesus meant with his lamp illustration?

2. How can we develop ears that hear what God has to say?

3. What do you think Jesus meant by "the measure" we use?

DAY FOUR READING AND QUESTIONS

²⁶He also said, "This is what the kingdom of God is like. A man scatter seed on the ground. ²⁷Night and day, whether he sleeps or gets up, the seed sprouts and grows, though he does not know how. ²⁸All by itself the soil produces grain—first the stalk, then the head, then the full kernel in the head. ²⁹As soon as the grain is ripe, he puts the sickle to it, because the harvest has come."

³⁰Again he said, "What shall we say the kingdom of God is like, or what parable shall we use to describe it? ³¹It is like a mustard seed, which is the smallest seed you plant in the ground. ³²Yet when planted, it grows and becomes the largest of all garden plants, with such big branches that the birds of the air can perch in its shade."

³³With many similar parables Jesus spoke the word to them, as much as they could understand. ³⁴ He did not say anything to them

without using a parable. But when he was alone with his own disciples, he explained everything.

1. What insight about the kingdom do you gain from these parables?

2. To what actions do these parables call us?

3. What do you think it would have been like to be one of the disciples when Jesus more fully explained his teaching?

DAY FIVE READING AND QUESTIONS

Reread the entire text (4:1-34).

1. How relevant do you perceive Jesus' parables to be today?

2. Mark tells us that Jesus used parables extensively. What might we learn from this?

3. How have you seen the truth of these parables in your life?

MEDITATION

How does one teach effectively, especially when one's audience is not prepared to hear what needs to be taught? Jesus was proclaiming a message of great interest to his hearers—the coming of the kingdom of God! Most of his audience thought they were experts on the topic. They rejoiced at the great power demonstrated by Jesus up to this point in his ministry. His ability to heal, to cast out demons, his authoritative teaching—all of this fit the people's hopes for the messianic kingdom. But their expectations were terribly misguided. They anticipated an earthly kingdom that would give them power and prominence on the world stage. How could Jesus help them realize their hopes were erroneous? In fact, their dreams for "kingdom" were too small! Jesus chose to confront this difficult teaching challenge by using stories—common stories to which his listeners could relate. We call them "parables."

A parable is a simple story that provides on opportunity for the listener to gain new insight or a deeper understanding. Jesus did not mask his intent. He wanted his listeners to comprehend the *true* nature of the kingdom of God. The kingdom was indeed powerful, but only for those who choose to open their hearts to God. Though the "seed" of the kingdom was and is amazingly potent, it will only produce fruit when planted in soil willing to receive it. The responsibility of allowing kingdom power to change our lives is squarely on our shoulders. The power is God's; the willingness to receive it is ours. Soil type for kingdom seed depends on the choices we make in our daily lives.

Jesus explained his use of parables by quoting Isaiah (6:9). To say the least, this passage has caused much discussion. How could it be that God does not want us to see and does not want us to hear? Why would he not want us to repent and be forgiven? How could it be that God would so encode the mystery of the kingdom that it could be deciphered by a chosen few? The passage is not to be taken literally; it is fine irony. It is not that God does not want us to perceive truth—it is that truth is so obvious *to those seeking* it that repentance is the only possible outcome. But truth is available only to those willing to receive it and allow it to germinate.

Jesus makes it clear that it is not God's intent to hide anything. Truth is like a lamp—you don't put it under your bed, rather, you put it on a stand for all to see. Let anyone who has ears to hear, hear! The invitation is to open our eyes to see and open our ears to hear. And when we do—watch out! Like a small mustard seed, kingdom life expands into a tree so large we can hardly comprehend it.

So, where are we in the growing tension of Mark's gospel? We have seen the miracles; we have heard the teaching. What is happening with the kingdom seed in our lives? Are we letting God do his work through us? Is our soil broken and ready? Will we hear the word, see the truth, repent and find life?

"Oh Lord, break the hard soil of my life. May the seed of kingdom truth sink deeply within and produce fruit that comes only by your power. It is amazing that you would count me worthy to receive the good news of your kingdom. May it yield much to your glory."

AMAZING POWER

(4:35-5:20)

DAY ONE READING AND QUESTIONS

[35]That day when evening came, he said to his disciples, "Let us go over to the other side." [36]Leaving the crowd behind, they took him along, just as he was, in the boat. There were also other boats with him. [37]A furious squall came up, and the waves broke over the boat, so that it was nearly swamped. [38]Jesus was in the stern, sleeping on a cushion. The disciples woke him and said to him, "Teacher, don't you care if we drown?"

[39]He got up, rebuked the wind and said to the waves, "Quiet! Be still!" Then the wind died down and it was completely calm.

[40]He said to his disciples, "Why are you so afraid? Do you still have no faith?"

[41]They were terrified and asked each other, "Who is this? Even the wind and the waves obey him!"

1. *How do you think Jesus felt at the end of a long, exhausting day of teaching?*

2. *Have you ever been in a storm while in a boat or ship? Reflect on the fear created by such an experience.*

3. *What would you have thought had you been there when Jesus calmed the storm? Why do you think the disciples were afraid instead of comforted?*

DAY TWO READING AND QUESTIONS

5:1They went across the lake to the region of the Gerasenes. 2When Jesus got out of the boat, a man with an evil spirit came from the tombs to meet him. 3This man lived in the tombs, and no one could bind him any more, not even with a chain. 4For he had often been chained hand and foot, but he tore the chains apart and broke the irons on his feet. No one was strong enough to subdue him. 5Night and day among the tombs and in the hills he would cry out and cut himself with stones.

6When he saw Jesus from a distance, he ran and fell on his knees in front of him. 7He shouted at the top of his voice, "What do you want with me, Jesus, Son of the Most High God? Swear to God that you won't torture me!" 8For Jesus had said to him, "Come out of this man, you evil spirit!"

9Then Jesus asked him, "What is your name?"

"My name is Legion," he replied, "for we are many." 10And he begged Jesus again and again not to send them out of the area.

1. *Imagine having been through the unnerving experience of a storm at sea only to arrive at such a scene as this. How do you think you would have responded?*

2. *Imagine what the demon possessed man must have looked like. What do you think the disciples were thinking as he ran towards them?*

3. *Why was Legion afraid of Jesus?*

DAY THREE READING AND QUESTIONS

11A large herd of pigs was feeding on the nearby hillside. 12The demons begged Jesus, "Send us among the pigs; allow us to go into them." 13He gave them permission, and the evil spirits came out and went into the pigs. The herd, about two thousand in number, rushed down the steep bank into the lake and were drowned.

[14]Those tending the pigs ran off and reported this in the town and countryside, and the people went out to see what had happened. [15]When they came to Jesus, they saw the man who had been possessed by the legion of demons, sitting there, dressed and in his right mind; and they were afraid. [16]Those who had seen it told the people what had happened to the demon-possessed man—and told about the pigs as well. [17]Then the people began to plead with Jesus to leave their region.

1. *Why do you think the demons wanted to go into the pigs?*

2. *What does the influence of the demons in the pigs show us about the desire of Satan for God's creation?*

3. *Why were the people afraid when they saw the formerly demon possessed man healed and in his right mind?*

DAY FOUR READING AND QUESTIONS

[18]As Jesus was getting into the boat, the man who had been demon-possessed begged to go with him. [19]Jesus did not let him, but said, "Go home to your family and tell them how much the Lord has done for you, and how he has had mercy on you." [20]So the man went away and began to tell in the Decapolis how much Jesus had done for him. And all the people were amazed.

1. *Why do you think the demon possessed man wanted to go with Jesus?*

2. *Why does Jesus not prohibit the man from telling of his miraculous cure, as he had prohibited others?*

3. *What was the message the man was to share?*

DAY FIVE READING AND QUESTIONS

Reread the entire text (4:35-5:20).

1. *What do you think Mark wants us to understand through this amazing story?*

2. *What does this story tell us about the power of Satan compared to the power of God?*

3. *Do we have a burning desire to tell of God's mercy for us? How can we develop a deeper understanding of his grace and forgiveness?*

MEDITATION

After a rough night at sea, the disciples arrived with Jesus to an unfamiliar shoreline. Finally away from the Galilean crowds, the disciples were probably anticipating a time of rest. As they got out of their boats, an alarming sight confronted them. A wild, torn, bleeding, and obviously tortured man ran right at Jesus. So much for a time of rest! He was screaming, "Jesus, Son of the Most High God, don't torture me!" If I were a disciple, I would want to know how that man knew Jesus' name. But why would this distressed man fear Jesus, the gentle healer? Why would he think Jesus might torture him? It wasn't the man who feared Jesus, but the army of demons who possessed him, and they knew they were in serious trouble with Jesus landing on their shore.

This confrontation raises unique questions. For example, why did the demons want to go into the pigs? We can only speculate. Apparently there was a worse fate than possessing a pig—being sent into the abyss, for one. Then, when given the permission to enter the pigs, they jumped off the cliff into the sea and drowned. Another question: escaping the abyss the demons jump into an abyss—why? Here we plainly see the ultimate plan of Satan. His only desire is to destroy the work of God's creation. When "Legion" was in the man, they had nearly destroyed his life, but they apparently could not end it. Might it be that humankind's innate "image of God" prohibited Satan from destroying him? When released to pigs, there was no resistance. Destruction was inevitable.

Some suggest the owners of the pigs were Jews, which would have been a violation of their law. But the text does not tell us this. The destruction of the pigs is not something which we should celebrate. It represents the desire of Satan to destroy God's creation.

One more question. Why were the people of the region afraid of Jesus? It ought to be clear by now—when one experiences the awesome power of Jesus, there is good reason to fear. I recently read a book which described Jesus as mean and wild at times rather than meek and mild. Which was he? Both. When people saw the amazing power available to him, they rightfully were terrified! Jesus was not "mean" in a destructive way or "wild" in a way that would question his integrity, but he did not hesitate to do what was necessary to stand for truth or demonstrate the power of God over evil.

There was one in the story who was not afraid. The one who was healed sat at the feet of Jesus, deeply grateful for his new life. He wanted to stay with Jesus, to follow him, to learn more from him. But this was not God's purpose. Jesus, in his ministry, would not return to these shores. So the healed man was given the privilege of being the first appointed evangelist in the gospel of Mark. He was to go tell all in the region about the mercy he had received. And so he did.

As we journey through Mark, we are confronted with stories that manifest the great power of Jesus. He was able to heal diseases, restore lifeless limbs, rebuild the muscles of the paralyzed, calm storms, and not only cast out demons but cast out armies of them. Satan had and has no power that can challenge the Son of God. This is an important truth. Satan did not defeat Jesus later in the story. Jesus laid down his life so that Satan would forever be defeated. Because of that victory, we cannot be overpowered by Satan. The only power he has in the life of the believer is the power the believer grants to him. His only hope is that we allow ourselves to be separated from Jesus, the victorious Son of God.

We have seen the healing power of Jesus. It has cleansed us. It has the power to turn us from our sins. We sit at his feet, healed of our diseases, and Jesus calls us to tell of his mercy to all we know.

"Lord, thank you for the healing you have given me. May I use my life to tell of your wondrous mercy. Remind me often that you have defeated Satan, and that he has no power over me if I am walking with you."

HEALING, REJECTION, AND MISSION

(5:21-6:13)

DAY ONE READING AND QUESTIONS

[21]When Jesus had again crossed over by boat to the other side of the lake, a large crowd gathered around him while he was by the lake. [22]Then one of the synagogue rulers, named Jairus, came there. Seeing Jesus, he fell at his feet [23]and pleaded earnestly with him, "My little daughter is dying. Please come and put your hands on her so that she will be healed and live." [24]So Jesus went with him.

A large crowd followed and pressed around him. [25]And a woman was there who had been subject to bleeding for twelve years. [26]She had suffered a great deal under the care of many doctors and had spent all she had, yet instead of getting better she grew worse. [27]When she heard about Jesus, she came up behind him in the crowd and touched his cloak, [28]because she thought, "If I just touch his clothes, I will be healed." [29]Immediately her bleeding stopped and she felt in her body that she was freed from her suffering.

[30]At once Jesus realized that power had gone out from him. He turned around in the crowd and asked, "Who touched my clothes?"

[31]"You see the people crowding against you," his disciples answered, "and yet you can ask, 'Who touched me?' "

[32]But Jesus kept looking around to see who had done it. [33] Then the woman, knowing what had happened to her, came and fell at his

feet and, trembling with fear, told him the whole truth. [34]He said to her, "Daughter, your faith has healed you. Go in peace and be freed from your suffering."

1. Why was Jairus, a synagogue ruler, willing to fall at Jesus' feet?

2. Why do you think the woman with the bleeding problem had so much faith in Jesus?

3. For whose sake did Jesus stop and bring attention to the healed woman?

DAY TWO READING AND QUESTIONS

[35]While Jesus was still speaking, some men came from the house of Jairus, the synagogue ruler. "Your daughter is dead," they said. "Why bother the teacher any more?"

[36]Ignoring what they said, Jesus told the synagogue ruler, "Don't be afraid; just believe."

[37]He did not let anyone follow him except Peter, James and John the brother of James. [38]When they came to the home of the synagogue ruler, Jesus saw a commotion, with people crying and wailing loudly. [39]He went in and said to them, "Why all this commotion and wailing? The child is not dead but asleep." [40]But they laughed at him.

After he put them all out, he took the child's father and mother and the disciples who were with him, and went in where the child was. [41]He took her by the hand and said to her, *"Talitha koum!"* (which means, "Little girl, I say to you, get up!"). [42]Immediately the girl stood up and walked around (she was twelve years old). At this they were completely astonished. [43]He gave strict orders not to let anyone know about this, and told them to give her something to eat.

1. Put yourself in the place of Jairus when he was told his daughter had died. Now hear Jesus say, "Don't be afraid; just believe." What do you think Jairus was experiencing?

2. *Why did the people laugh at Jesus when he proclaimed the little girl was "sleeping"?*

3. *Why did Mark include the detail about giving the newly resurrected girl something to eat?*

DAY THREE READING AND QUESTIONS

⁶:¹Jesus left there and went to his hometown, accompanied by his disciples. ²When the Sabbath came, he began to teach in the synagogue, and many who heard him were amazed.

"Where did this man get these things?" they asked. "What's this wisdom that has been given him, that he even does miracles! ³Isn't this the carpenter? Isn't this Mary's son and the brother of James, Joseph, Judas and Simon? Aren't his sisters here with us?" And they took offense at him.

⁴Jesus said to them, "Only in his hometown, among his relatives and in his own house is a prophet without honor." ⁵He could not do any miracles there, except lay his hands on a few sick people and heal them. ⁶And he was amazed at their lack of faith.

1. *Why would wisdom and miracles be connected in the minds of those in Nazareth?*

2. *Why would the people of Nazareth take offense at Jesus?*

3. *What do you think is the connection between the people's lack of faith and Jesus not performing many miracles?*

DAY FOUR READING AND QUESTIONS

Then Jesus went around teaching from village to village. ⁷Calling the Twelve to him, he sent them out two by two and gave them authority over evil spirits.

[8]These were his instructions: "Take nothing for the journey except a staff—no bread, no bag, no money in your belts. [9]Wear sandals but not an extra tunic. [10]Whenever you enter a house, stay there until you leave that town. [11]And if any place will not welcome you or listen to you, shake the dust off your feet when you leave, as a testimony against them."

[12]They went out and preached that people should repent. [13]They drove out many demons and anointed many sick people with oil and healed them.

1. Why did Jesus send his disciples "two by two"?

2. Why were the disciples to go out without provisions for the journey?

3. Why do you think Jesus instructed them to stay at one house until they moved to the next town?

DAY FIVE READING AND QUESTIONS

Reread the entire text (5:21-6:13).

1. How do you generally view interruptions to your schedule? Might such a moment be a God-created opportunity to serve?

2. Have you ever faced rejection like Jesus did at Nazareth? How did you respond?

3. Does Jesus still "send us out?" How and why?

MEDITATION

I cannot imagine how difficult a moment it must have been for Jarius. He was desperate. Though a ruler of the synagogue, any sense of pride or elite social standing was thrown aside as he fell at Jesus' feet and pleaded "earnestly" for his daughter's life. I can picture him pulling Jesus through the crowd, one arm pulling Jesus, the other clearing the way. There was no time to waste. But Jesus came to a halt. He turned and asked, "Who touched me?" What do you think Jarius was thinking at this point? We know what the disciples' thought: "How could Jesus ask such an irrational question with so many crowding around him and a life at stake?" In spite of Jarius' urgent need, in the midst of the crowding mass, Jesus stopped. He stopped because a woman needed to understand what had happened to her. It was not enough that she was healed—it was important for her to know why. Jesus wanted her to experience the blessing of believing in God. Her healing was not magic. It wasn't the robe of Jesus that made her whole. It was her faith in the power of God. So Jesus gave her the great blessing of God's peace by acknowledging her faith. Once again, we encounter authentic faith in an unexpected place!

Jesus' willingness to serve the needs of an unknown woman had disastrous consequences—or so thought Jairus. His precious daughter died as Jesus paused to speak with the woman, so there was no need to bother "the teacher" any longer. The teacher? The teacher? They did not yet see him for who he was. You might let a teacher move on when death occurs, but not the Author of Life! So Jesus turned and spoke some of the most challenging words of his ministry, "Do not fear, but believe." Mark did not intend for this to be an isolated historical happening. These are words Jesus speaks every day to those who follow Him. These words are a way of life. There is no place for fear in the kingdom as one walks with Jesus Christ.

What do you think Jairus experienced when Jesus called his precious daughter back to life? Whether young or old, when one dies in the kingdom, it is merely sleep. If we die before he returns, we will someday hear his voice call us back to life. Therefore, with great confidence and unshakable faith we stand boldly in the face of pain and death, hearing the precious words of Jesus, "Do not fear, but believe."

"Lord of life, thank you for your heart for the hurting. Thank you for the gift of God's peace which you generously pour into our hearts. Thank you for our victory over the grave. Please give us a bold faith that removes all our fears."

A TRAGIC DEATH AND AN AMAZING FEAST

(6 2:14-44)

DAY ONE READING AND QUESTIONS

¹⁴King Herod heard about this, for Jesus' name had become well known. Some were saying, "John the Baptist has been raised from the dead, and that is why miraculous powers are at work in him."

¹⁵Others said, "He is Elijah." And still others claimed, "He is a prophet, like one of the prophets of long ago."

¹⁶But when Herod heard this, he said, "John, the man I beheaded, has been raised from the dead!"

¹⁷For Herod himself had given orders to have John arrested, and he had him bound and put in prison. He did this because of Herodias, his brother Philip's wife, whom he had married. ¹⁸For John had been saying to Herod, "It is not lawful for you to have your brother's wife." ¹⁹So Herodias nursed a grudge against John and wanted to kill him. But she was not able to, ²⁰because Herod feared John and protected him, knowing him to be a righteous and holy man. When Herod heard John, he was greatly puzzled; yet he liked to listen to him.

²¹Finally the opportune time came. On his birthday Herod gave a banquet for his high officials and military commanders and the leading men of Galilee. ²²When the daughter of Herodias came in and danced, she pleased Herod and his dinner guests.

1. Why did people associate Jesus with John the Baptist?

2. From what we know of John the Baptist, why did he confront Herod's sin?

3. Why do you think Herod liked listening to John?

DAY TWO READING AND QUESTIONS

The king said to the girl, "Ask me for anything you want, and I'll give it to you." ²³And he promised her with an oath, "Whatever you ask I will give you, up to half my kingdom."

²⁴She went out and said to her mother, "What shall I ask for?"

"The head of John the Baptist," she answered.

²⁵At once the girl hurried in to the king with the request: "I want you to give me right now the head of John the Baptist on a platter."

²⁶The king was greatly distressed, but because of his oaths and his dinner guests, he did not want to refuse her. ²⁷So he immediately sent an executioner with orders to bring John's head. The man went, beheaded John in the prison, ²⁸and brought back his head on a platter. He presented it to the girl, and she gave it to her mother. ²⁹On hearing of this, John's disciples came and took his body and laid it in a tomb.

1. What can we learn from Herod concerning rash promises?

2. What does the request of Herodias tell us of the life she was living?

3. Does the manner of the death of John the Baptist influence your understanding of life in the purposes of God? Why or why not?

DAY THREE READING AND QUESTIONS

³⁰The apostles gathered around Jesus and reported to him all they had done and taught. ³¹Then, because so many people were coming

and going that they did not even have a chance to eat, he said to them, "Come with me by yourselves to a quiet place and get some rest."

[32]So they went away by themselves in a boat to a solitary place. [33]But many who saw them leaving recognized them and ran on foot from all the towns and got there ahead of them. [34]When Jesus landed and saw a large crowd, he had compassion on them, because they were like sheep without a shepherd. So he began teaching them many things.

1. *About what were the apostles reporting to Jesus?*

2. *What does Jesus' idea of retreating and resting tell us about a life of ministry?*

3. *Even though Jesus and his followers needed rest, what did he do as the crowds once again reassembled? What does this tell us about Jesus?*

DAY FOUR READING AND QUESTIONS

[35]By this time it was late in the day, so his disciples came to him. "This is a remote place," they said, "and it's already very late. [36]Send the people away so they can go to the surrounding countryside and villages and buy themselves something to eat."

[37]But he answered, "You give them something to eat." They said to him, "That would take eight months of a man's wages ! Are we to go and spend that much on bread and give it to them to eat?"

[38]"How many loaves do you have?" he asked. "Go and see." When they found out, they said, "Five—and two fish."

[39]Then Jesus directed them to have all the people sit down in groups on the green grass. [40]So they sat down in groups of hundreds and fifties. [41]Taking the five loaves and the two fish and looking up to heaven, he gave thanks and broke the loaves. Then he gave them to his disciples to set before the people. He also divided the two fish among them all. [42]They all ate and were satisfied, [43]and the disciples

picked up twelve basketfuls of broken pieces of bread and fish. ⁴⁴The number of the men who had eaten was five thousand.

1. *Do you think the disciples' concern was legitimate? Why or why not?*

2. *How would you have felt had you been a disciple when Jesus said, "You feed them?"*

3. *How does this amazing miracle of feeding the five thousand influence your understanding of life in the kingdom of God?*

DAY FIVE READING AND QUESTIONS

Reread the entire text (6:14-44).

1. *What lessons can we learn from the life of John the Baptist?*

2. *Why do you think Jesus always thought about others first (here, the crowds)? How can we develop that spirit of service?*

3. *How can we learn to confront the challenges before us, not by our limitations, but with the power of God?*

MEDITATION

Surely the tragic end of John's life profoundly influences every reader of Mark's gospel. It is almost impossible to imagine a more unexpected turn of events. How could this be? The one who came as God's special messenger to prepare the way of the Messiah meets death at the request of a wicked woman seeking vengeance because her feelings were hurt? The story of John's death calls us to be aware that, though we are living fully in the purposes of God, we are not exempt from the influences of evil in the world. Such stories serve to save us from the simplistic expectation that if we are faithful to God, he is obliged to give us a life of comfort and happiness.

As Mark informs us of this tragic happening, Jesus' disciples were returning from their recent kingdom mission. Jesus recognized their need to get away from the crowds to rest and discuss their experiences. So they took a boat to a deserted place. But Jesus was so popular the crowds arrived before he did. What did Jesus do? Rather than be annoyed at their persistence, he was filled with compassion for their needs. I can't help but wonder what the disciples must have thought. We know it didn't take long until they wanted Jesus to send the crowds away so that all could eat. I would love to have seen the disciples' reaction to Jesus' suggestion, "You feed them." "You want us to feed five thousand men? That's a lot of sandwiches!" To make matters worse, all they could come up with was five loaves of bread and two fish. The kingdom of God is like a mustard seed, remember? It only takes a little in the hands of Jesus to become a huge blessing to a hungry world.

What will we take from this reading? A tragic, unexplainable death—the needless end of a great man's life—for what? An amazing, unexpected miracle—the feeding of thousands with a small sack lunch. How do we know how to act? How can we know if we will be victims of senseless violence or recipients of unexpected blessings? We can't. What is important is the realization that ultimately it doesn't matter. Our responsibility is to be faithful to God's calling. God takes care of the rest.

"Father of all living things and creator of the universe, use me to your glory and praise. Give me the strength to be faithful to your call."

WHOM WILL YOU OBEY?

(6:45-7:23)

DAY ONE READING AND QUESTIONS

⁴⁵Immediately Jesus made his disciples get into the boat and go on ahead of him to Bethsaida, while he dismissed the crowd. ⁴⁶After leaving them, he went up on a mountainside to pray.

⁴⁷When evening came, the boat was in the middle of the lake, and he was alone on land. ⁴⁸He saw the disciples straining at the oars, because the wind was against them. About the fourth watch of the night he went out to them, walking on the lake. He was about to pass by them, ⁴⁹but when they saw him walking on the lake, they thought he was a ghost. They cried out, ⁵⁰because they all saw him and were terrified.

Immediately he spoke to them and said, "Take courage! It is I. Don't be afraid." ⁵¹Then he climbed into the boat with them, and the wind died down. They were completely amazed, ⁵²for they had not understood about the loaves; their hearts were hardened.

⁵³When they had crossed over, they landed at Gennesaret and anchored there. ⁵⁴As soon as they got out of the boat, people recognized Jesus. ⁵⁵They ran throughout that whole region and carried the sick on mats to wherever they heard he was. ⁵⁶And wherever he went—into villages, towns or countryside—they placed the sick in the marketplaces. They begged him to let them touch even the edge of his cloak, and all who touched him were healed.

1. Why do you think Jesus prayed so often?

2. What should the disciples have understood about Jesus when they saw him walking on water?

3. What does his walking on the water have to do with the disciples' understanding of the loaves (why does Mark's gospel connect the two)?

DAY TWO READING AND QUESTIONS

[7:1]The Pharisees and some of the teachers of the law who had come from Jerusalem gathered around Jesus and [2]saw some of his disciples eating food with hands that were "unclean," that is, unwashed. [3](The Pharisees and all the Jews do not eat unless they give their hands a ceremonial washing, holding to the tradition of the elders. [4]When they come from the marketplace they do not eat unless they wash. And they observe many other traditions, such as the washing of cups, pitchers and kettles.)

[5]So the Pharisees and teachers of the law asked Jesus, "Why don't your disciples live according to the tradition of the elders instead of eating their food with 'unclean' hands?"

[6]He replied, "Isaiah was right when he prophesied about you hypocrites; as it is written:

" 'These people honor me with their lips,
      but their hearts are far from me.
[7]They worship me in vain;
      their teachings are but rules taught by men.'

[8]You have let go of the commands of God and are holding on to the traditions of men."

1. Why does Mark give us so much information about "washing"?

2. How did the "teaching of the elders" affect the way the Pharisees valued others?

3. How were the Pharisees letting go of what God commanded?

DAY THREE READING AND QUESTIONS

[9]And he said to them: "You have a fine way of setting aside the commands of God in order to observe your own traditions! [10]For Moses said, 'Honor your father and your mother,' and, 'Anyone who curses his father or mother must be put to death.' [11]But you say that if a man says to his father or mother: 'Whatever help you might otherwise have received from me is Corban' (that is, a gift devoted to God), [12]then you no longer let him do anything for his father or mother. [13]Thus you nullify the word of God by your tradition that you have handed down. And you do many things like that."

[14]Again Jesus called the crowd to him and said, "Listen to me, everyone, and understand this. [15]Nothing outside a man can make him 'unclean' by going into him. Rather, it is what comes out of a man that makes him 'unclean.'"

1. What example did Jesus use to demonstrate how they were using traditions to violate the will of God?

2. Why is it important that we honor our parents?

3. What makes one unclean and why?

DAY FOUR READING AND QUESTIONS

[17]After he had left the crowd and entered the house, his disciples asked him about this parable. [18]"Are you so dull?" he asked. "Don't you see that nothing that enters a man from the outside can make him 'unclean'? [19]For it doesn't go into his heart but into his stomach, and then out of his body." (In saying this, Jesus declared all foods "clean.")

[20]He went on: "What comes out of a man is what makes him 'unclean.' [21]For from within, out of men's hearts, come evil thoughts, sexual immorality, theft, murder, adultery, [22]greed, malice, deceit,

lewdness, envy, slander, arrogance and folly. [23]All these evils come from inside and make a man 'unclean.' "

1. Why do you think the disciples were confused about Jesus' teaching concerning what makes one unclean?

2. How is it that evils come from inside?

3. What thoughts do you battle which might make you "unclean"?

DAY FIVE READING AND QUESTIONS.

Reread the entire text (6:45-7:23)

1. How should Jesus' life of prayer (prayer practices) influence us?

2. Have you known of religious traditions in your experience that have led people away from the purposes of God? How can we keep this from happening?

3. How do we win the battle of "wrong thinking" (thinking about things that lead to sin)?

MEDITATION

The miracles of Jesus continue to demonstrate not only his power, but his identity. Jesus had just fed the five thousand. It should have been obvious, especially to his disciples, that this was a messianic event. Yet again we encounter their lack of faith. Jesus sent his disciples ahead of him across the lake as he withdrew for a night of prayer (again). The disciples encountered a strong head wind and were struggling to make headway. The text provides little information as to why, but Jesus walked out to them during early morning hours. Understandably, they were terrified to see, in the darkness, one walking on water. Jesus calmed their fears by identifying himself. He entered the boat and the wind ceased. They were "completely amazed."

This amazement was not an expression of praise, but of great surprise. Mark informs us this was because they had not understood the meaning of feeding the multitude. If they had comprehended that the sovereign Lord was the only one who could feed five thousand with five loaves and two fish, they would not have been surprised to see him walk on water. Who do you think they thought he was? Perhaps the more important question is for us, "Who do we think Jesus is?" It is the answer to this question that determines our willingness to submit our lives fully to him.

After a wonderful paragraph telling of many healings by the dynamic power of the living God, we once again encounter the lifeless religion of the Pharisees. While Jesus was concerned with the sick, diseased, maimed and blind, the experts of the law were preoccupied with their own purity (separation from anything unclean). Jesus reminds us of the danger of such a focus—it often leads into disobedience. When we are more concerned with personal piety than helping the hurting, our hearts are out of tune with God's song of life. We can even use our rule-keeping as an excuse to violate the will of God, as did the religious authorities of Jesus day with their view of "Corban."

The real question is not whether we submit to the external purification rituals of religion, but whether our hearts are submitted to God. What occupies our minds? About what do we choose to think? Might it be possible that, just as with the Pharisees of Jesus' day, our religious rituals serve as cover for unrepentant hearts? Being clean starts with a transformed heart. The external practices of religion only have meaning when they are manifestations of a change of heart.

"Sovereign Lord, may we see you for who you are. Change us from within that we might be truly clean and holy—set apart for your purposes."

FAITH—THOSE WITH AND THOSE WITHOUT

(7:24-8:21)

DAY ONE READING AND QUESTIONS

²⁴Jesus left that place and went to the vicinity of Tyre. He entered a house and did not want anyone to know it; yet he could not keep his presence secret. ²⁵In fact, as soon as she heard about him, a woman whose little daughter was possessed by an evil spirit came and fell at his feet. ²⁶The woman was a Greek, born in Syrian Phoenicia. She begged Jesus to drive the demon out of her daughter.

²⁷"First let the children eat all they want," he told her, "for it is not right to take the children's bread and toss it to their dogs."

²⁸"Yes, Lord," she replied, "but even the dogs under the table eat the children's crumbs."

²⁹Then he told her, "For such a reply, you may go; the demon has left your daughter."

³⁰She went home and found her child lying on the bed, and the demon gone.

1. Why was Jesus trying to hide from people?

2. Why did Jesus suggest it would not be appropriate for him to help the woman?

3. Why did the Greek woman's reply please Jesus?

69

DAY TWO READING AND QUESTIONS

[31]Then Jesus left the vicinity of Tyre and went through Sidon, down to the Sea of Galilee and into the region of the Decapolis. [32]There some people brought to him a man who was deaf and could hardly talk, and they begged him to place his hand on the man.

[33]After he took him aside, away from the crowd, Jesus put his fingers into the man's ears. Then he spit and touched the man's tongue. [34]He looked up to heaven and with a deep sigh said to him, *"Ephphatha!"* (which means, "Be opened!"). [35]At this, the man's ears were opened, his tongue was loosened and he began to speak plainly.

[36]Jesus commanded them not to tell anyone. But the more he did so, the more they kept talking about it. [37]People were overwhelmed with amazement. "He has done everything well," they said. "He even makes the deaf hear and the mute speak."

1. Why was Jesus' fame continuing to spread?

2. Why do you think Jesus sighed as he looked to heaven?

3. Why did people not keep quiet about the healings, as Jesus requested?

DAY THREE READING AND QUESTIONS

[8:1]During those days another large crowd gathered. Since they had nothing to eat, Jesus called his disciples to him and said, [2]"I have compassion for these people; they have already been with me three days and have nothing to eat. [3]If I send them home hungry, they will collapse on the way, because some of them have come a long distance."

[4]His disciples answered, "But where in this remote place can anyone get enough bread to feed them?"

[5]"How many loaves do you have?" Jesus asked. "Seven," they replied.

⁶He told the crowd to sit down on the ground. When he had taken the seven loaves and given thanks, he broke them and gave them to his disciples to set before the people, and they did so. ⁷They had a few small fish as well; he gave thanks for them also and told the disciples to distribute them. ⁸The people ate and were satisfied. Afterward the disciples picked up seven basketfuls of broken pieces that were left over. ⁹About four thousand men were present. And having sent them away, ¹⁰he got into the boat with his disciples and went to the region of Dalmanutha.

¹¹The Pharisees came and began to question Jesus. To test him, they asked him for a sign from heaven. ¹²He sighed deeply and said, "Why does this generation ask for a miraculous sign? I tell you the truth, no sign will be given to it." ¹³Then he left them, got back into the boat and crossed to the other side.

1. *What caused people to follow Jesus even at the expense of not eating for days at a time?*

2. *How do you think the disciples should have responded to Jesus' suggestion that the crowd needed to eat?*

3. *Why did Jesus react negatively to the Pharisees' request for a sign from heaven?*

DAY FOUR READING AND QUESTIONS

¹⁴The disciples had forgotten to bring bread, except for one loaf they had with them in the boat. ¹⁵"Be careful," Jesus warned them. "Watch out for the yeast of the Pharisees and that of Herod."

¹⁶They discussed this with one another and said, "It is because we have no bread."

¹⁷Aware of their discussion, Jesus asked them: "Why are you talking about having no bread? Do you still not see or understand?

71

Are your hearts hardened? [18]Do you have eyes but fail to see, and ears but fail to hear? And don't you remember? [19]When I broke the five loaves for the five thousand, how many basketfuls of pieces did you pick up?" "Twelve," they replied.

[20]"And when I broke the seven loaves for the four thousand, how many basketfuls of pieces did you pick up?" They answered, "Seven."

[21]He said to them, "Do you still not understand?"

1. *When Jesus mentioned "yeast," what does the disciples reaction tell us about their hearts and minds?*

2. *Why did Jesus quiz them about the two feedings of the multitudes?*

3. *Why do you think the disciples were so dull in their ability to understand what Jesus was doing and saying?*

DAY FIVE READING AND QUESTIONS

Reread the entire text (7:24-8:21).

1. *How does the Syrphoenician woman demonstrate deep faith? What can we learn from her?*

2. *How should Jesus' signs and miracles affect our understanding of him?*

3. *Are you sometimes so saturated with thoughts about the material world that spiritual truths are inaccessible? What can we do to avoid this?*

MEDITATION

This week's reading continues to portray the battle of authentic and inauthentic spirituality in a powerful way. The story of Jesus' interaction with the Syrophoenician woman has caused some distress. How could Jesus, with his kind and compassionate heart, tell a woman that her concern for her child was not worthy of his attention? Much has been written trying to soften the words of Jesus. They are recorded so that we might see the beauty of authentic faith. Jesus was expressing his specific mission: to take the good news of the kingdom to the children of God (Israel). He stated this in an unambiguous way to the Greek woman. Rather than be offended, she chose to acknowledge the wisdom of God in what Jesus was doing. It was her act of submitting to God's will that allowed her to receive the blessing she sought. It is painful to compare her sweet, submissive, unassuming spirit to the hardened hearts of the disciples—or, to the real point, to compare her sweet spirit of submission to my own belligerent heart.

How many healings, how many manifestations of power over creation, what would Jesus have to do to convince his disciples who he really was? Now we add to the list Jesus healing a deaf mute. I love the description of his work by those who observed him: "He has done everything well." It is in the immediate context of this miracle that we find Jesus and his disciples in a familiar place. Growing crowds, days without food, in the wilderness—time for a simple test. What have the disciples learned? Bigger question: what have we learned?

Jesus gave them the chance to redeem themselves. "These people need food." How should they have responded? "Lord, we have little, but we know you can feed these people with what we have. We have seen you do it before." But, no, they still did not understand. They failed the test. Once again we hear the echoes of empty and hardened hearts: "Where will we get enough bread?" Some have suggested Mark recorded two versions of the same miracle, with slightly different numbers. Those who propose this miss one of the main teachings of Mark's gospel. This is a story that challenges us to believe in Jesus as the Son of God. Are we learning about our own lives in the context of God's kingdom as we read of the disciples' continuing failure to understand? Once again the Messianic banquet is served—and once again there is more than can be eaten! Do we now believe?

So what happens next? The Pharisees want a sign from heaven! What more needs to be done? Do we not see? Faith based on sight is not faith. There are not enough miracles in the world to force a non-believing heart into belief. The Pharisees chose not to believe. Picture Jesus deep in troubled thought after this exchange with religious authorities. See him in a boat with his disciples, struggling to make sense of such belligerent hearts. Hear his ominous warning as he bowed his head and shook it in disbelief, "Watch out for the yeast of the Pharisees and that of Herod." Then hear our own voices say in response, "Yes, you are right. We forgot to go to the grocery and buy sack lunches." How can we think this way? It is easy to condemn the disciples for their lack of understanding, but we have far fewer excuses than they. We know of the risen Lord who has given us our every need. But we still can't hear his warning against the perilous life of self-focused, bread-centered living. How many basketsful of bread were left over?

"Lord, be patient with us as we learn to acknowledge you as the provider of our daily needs. You have filled our baskets to overflowing. May we stay far away from the yeast of worldly concerns."

THE GIFT OF SIGHT TO THE BLIND

(8:22-9:1)

DAY ONE READING AND QUESTIONS

²²They came to Bethsaida, and some people brought a blind man and begged Jesus to touch him. ²³He took the blind man by the hand and led him outside the village. When he had spit on the man's eyes and put his hands on him, Jesus asked, "Do you see anything?"

²⁴He looked up and said, "I see people; they look like trees walking around."

²⁵Once more Jesus put his hands on the man's eyes. Then his eyes were opened, his sight was restored, and he saw everything clearly. ²⁶Jesus sent him home, saying, "Don't go into the village.'"

1. *Why do you think Jesus took the blind man out of the village before the healing?*

2. *Why do you think a second touch was needed in order to give the man sight?*

3. *Can you think of events in your life that required a "second touch" before you fully understood their meaning?*

DAY TWO READING AND QUESTIONS

²⁷Jesus and his disciples went on to the villages around Caesarea Philippi. On the way he asked them, "Who do people say I am?"

²⁸They replied, "Some say John the Baptist; others say Elijah; and still others, one of the prophets."

²⁹"But what about you?" he asked. "Who do you say I am?"

Peter answered, "You are the Christ.'"

³⁰Jesus warned them not to tell anyone about him.

1. *Imagine you knew nothing of Jesus other than what you have learned in Mark's gospel to this point. How would you respond if Jesus asked, "Who do you say I am?"*

2. *Do you find surprising the answers people gave concerning who Jesus was? Why didn't they, like Peter, acknowledge Jesus as the Christ?*

3. *Why do you think Jesus did not want it told that he was the Christ?*

DAY THREE READING AND QUESTIONS

³¹He then began to teach them that the Son of Man must suffer many things and be rejected by the elders, chief priests and teachers of the law, and that he must be killed and after three days rise again. ³²He spoke plainly about this, and Peter took him aside and began to rebuke him.

³³But when Jesus turned and looked at his disciples, he rebuked Peter. "Get behind me, Satan!" he said. "You do not have in mind the things of God, but the things of men."

1. *Why would Jesus wait till this time to teach that he was to be killed but would rise again?*

2. *Why would Peter rebuke Jesus for telling of his death?*

3. *Why did Jesus call Peter "Satan"?*

DAY FOUR READING AND QUESTIONS

³⁴Then he called the crowd to him along with his disciples and said: "If anyone would come after me, he must deny himself and take

up his cross and follow me. [35]For whoever wants to save his life will lose it, but whoever loses his life for me and for the gospel will save it. [36]What good is it for a man to gain the whole world, yet forfeit his soul? [37]Or what can a man give in exchange for his soul? [38]If anyone is ashamed of me and my words in this adulterous and sinful generation, the Son of Man will be ashamed of him when he comes in his Father's glory with the holy angels." [9:1]And he said to them, "I tell you the truth, some who are standing here will not taste death before they see the kingdom of God come with power."

1. *When Jesus said, "If anyone would come after me," where do you think the disciples anticipated this would lead?*

2. *Is it true that one who wants to save his life will lose it? How so?*

3. *Why would anyone be ashamed of the words of Jesus?*

DAY FIVE READING AND QUESTIONS

Reread the entire text (8:22-9:1).

1. *Some suggest this reading contains the heart of the message of authentic discipleship. Do you think it does? If so, what is the central call of Jesus to each of us?*

2. *Peter argued when Jesus foretold his death. Have you ever argued with Jesus about the script of your life?*

3. *What are things we might mistakenly give in exchange for our lives? How can we help one another recognize what is truly meaningful in life?*

MEDITATION

This reading brings us to the first climax of Mark's gospel. All that Jesus had said and done brought him to the question, "Who do people say that I am?" Obviously all were impressed with Jesus. But they were not ready to proclaim him Messiah. Peter was. His voice rang out confidently, "You are the Christ."

It seems that the second touch in the healing of the blind man serves to remind us that just because we think we can see does not mean we see things accurately. The second touch healing serves as a "hinge" for what has happened up to this point in the story and for what is to come. Should we not (or the disciples, with whom we most easily identify as we read the story of Jesus' life) by this point in the story know who Jesus is? The blind man was given sight, but only with the second touch did he see accurately. Finally, after multiple miracles and amazing signs, we are ready to acknowledge Jesus as the Christ—but do we really know what that means?

Peter was excited and proud to proclaim Jesus was indeed the Christ, but Peter's understanding of what that meant was deeply flawed. What is our understanding? Jesus' "second touch" is one we *still* need to experience. He clearly instructed the disciples that, as the Christ, he would suffer many things and be killed. Peter could not believe it! He was confident he knew the script for the Christ. In the context of the recent events, as the picture of who Jesus was became clearer, Peter's imagination had doubtlessly rehearsed it many times. The messianic story should end in a victory parade in Jerusalem, not death! Peter was so sure of himself that he took Jesus aside to correct him! Can you imagine?

Before we are too hard on Peter, we need to take a long look at how we see our own lives. Do we, at times, insist on Jesus coming with us where we want to go rather than following him to the cross? Are we like Peter in that we are thinking of the things of this world rather than the things of God? Here is the heart of the good news of Jesus: we must give up making our lives what we want them to be. That is what it means to "deny self." It is time to fully surrender the ego and pick up a radically different image for our lives. Rather than the throne of self, we are called to pick up the cross. Only then are we authentic disciples. Only then can we find real life.

If we continue living for self, even if we could gain the entire world, of what benefit is that? It is nothing. If we are seeking for true meaning in life, it is only found on the other side of death. Not physical death, but death of self. If we want to find life, we must lose it. Will we believe? Or will we be ashamed and turn away? Do we acknowledge Jesus as the Christ? Are we willing to pay the price required by such a confession? Will we receive the "second touch" and see the life of sacrifice to which we have been called?

"Dear Lord, give us the courage and the faith to allow you to clarify our vision of the life to which you call us. May we be willing, daily, to deny ourselves and pick up the life of sacrifice to which you call us."

THE TRANSFIGURATION

(9:2-29)

DAY ONE READING AND QUESTIONS

²After six days Jesus took Peter, James and John with him and led them up a high mountain, where they were all alone. There he was transfigured before them. ³His clothes became dazzling white, whiter than anyone in the world could bleach them. ⁴And there appeared before them Elijah and Moses, who were talking with Jesus.

⁵Peter said to Jesus, "Rabbi, it is good for us to be here. Let us put up three shelters—one for you, one for Moses and one for Elijah." ⁶(He did not know what to say, they were so frightened.)

⁷Then a cloud appeared and enveloped them, and a voice came from the cloud: "This is my Son, whom I love. Listen to him!"

1. Take a moment and try to imagine experiencing the transfiguration. What do you think it would have been like?

2. What do you think Peter intended when he suggested building shelters?

3. What was God's message to the disciples and to us?

DAY TWO READING AND QUESTIONS

⁸Suddenly, when they looked around, they no longer saw anyone with them except Jesus.

[9]As they were coming down the mountain, Jesus gave them orders not to tell anyone what they had seen until the Son of Man had risen from the dead. [10]They kept the matter to themselves, discussing what "rising from the dead" meant.

[11]And they asked him, "Why do the teachers of the law say that Elijah must come first?"

[12]Jesus replied, "To be sure, Elijah does come first, and restores all things. Why then is it written that the Son of Man must suffer much and be rejected? [13]But I tell you, Elijah has come, and they have done to him everything they wished, just as it is written about him."

1. *Why did Jesus order them not to speak of this event until after his resurrection?*

2. *Why do you think the disciples asked about Elijah on the way down the mountain?*

3. *To what did Jesus' comments about the treatment of Elijah point?*

DAY THREE READING AND QUESTIONS

[14]When they came to the other disciples, they saw a large crowd around them and the teachers of the law arguing with them. [15]As soon as all the people saw Jesus, they were overwhelmed with wonder and ran to greet him.

[16]"What are you arguing with them about?" he asked.

[17]A man in the crowd answered, "Teacher, I brought you my son, who is possessed by a spirit that has robbed him of speech. [18]Whenever it seizes him, it throws him to the ground. He foams at the mouth, gnashes his teeth and becomes rigid. I asked your disciples to drive out the spirit, but they could not."

[19]"O unbelieving generation," Jesus replied, "how long shall I stay with you? How long shall I put up with you? Bring the boy to me."

[20]So they brought him. When the spirit saw Jesus, it immediately threw the boy into a convulsion. He fell to the ground and rolled around, foaming at the mouth.

[21]Jesus asked the boy's father, "How long has he been like this?" "From childhood," he answered. [22]"It has often thrown him into fire or water to kill him. But if you can do anything, take pity on us and help us."

[23]"'If you can'?" said Jesus. "Everything is possible for him who believes."

[24]Immediately the boy's father exclaimed, "I do believe; help me overcome my unbelief!"

1. *What do you think the "teachers of the law" were arguing with the disciples about concerning the man's son?*

2. *What does Jesus' response tell us about the problem confronting his disciples in their inability to cast out the demon?*

3. *Why did Jesus question the man's faith?*

DAY FOUR READING AND QUESTIONS

[25]When Jesus saw that a crowd was running to the scene, he rebuked the evil spirit. "You deaf and mute spirit," he said, "I command you, come out of him and never enter him again."

[26]The spirit shrieked, convulsed him violently and came out. The boy looked so much like a corpse that many said, "He's dead." [27]But Jesus took him by the hand and lifted him to his feet, and he stood up.

[28]After Jesus had gone indoors, his disciples asked him privately, "Why couldn't we drive it out?"[29]He replied, "This kind can come out only by prayer.'"

1. *How did the crowd influence what Jesus did?*

2. *Why do you think the evil spirit shrieked as it came out?*

3. What does Jesus' response to the disciples (when indoors and alone with them) tell us of their lack of power?

DAY FIVE READING AND QUESTIONS

Reread the entire text (9:2-29).

1. How should the story of Jesus' transfiguration affect our understanding of him?

2. Have you had "mountain top" experiences of faith only to almost immediately be forced to confront unbelief? How do you respond?

3. What can we learn from Jesus on how to respond to others' lack of belief?

MEDITATION

Peter's proclamation of Jesus as Messiah served as the first plot climax in Mark's gospel. The transfiguration affirms Jesus' identity beyond any doubt. What a moment! It is difficult to imagine how dramatic that experience must have been for the disciples—both terrifying and exhilarating at the same time. Surely this was what Peter had envisioned when he acknowledged his belief in Jesus as the Messiah. Could it be that the kingdom of God had begun? They were, after all, on a mountain top with Moses and Elijah! What else could be going on?

Peter did not know what to say, but surprisingly, what he did say made sense. If the kingdom was about to begin then Moses, Elijah, and Jesus would need places to stay. Peter was acknowledging his willingness to do whatever necessary to help them in the establishment of the kingdom. But another message was to be learned on that day, the message Mark is most intent on sharing: "Jesus is the Son of God." He is the full message from God. He is the fulfillment of all that God had done through the Law (Moses) and the prophets (Elijah). It is the voice of Jesus they were to hear and obey. It is the voice of Jesus that we must hear and obey. That is the essence of the kingdom of God.

This event, more than any other in his ministry, confirmed who Jesus was. Not only was he gloriously transfigured, but affirmed as the beloved Son by the voice of God himself. The three disciples with Jesus were instructed not to speak of this. I wonder whether that was easy or difficult. If they shared it, who would believe them? Yet, how could they not speak of such a glorious sight? I wonder if Peter felt vindicated—thinking that his version of Messiah was correct after all (remember Jesus' rebuke in 8:33).

From the mountaintop of glory to the valley of unbelief—Jesus was immediately confronted with the problem that continues to impact his church to this day. The disciples who had not accompanied Jesus up the mountain found themselves powerless to do his work in his absence. Jesus' response identified the problem: "O unbelieving generation, how long shall I stay with you?" They were attempting to cast out a demon by their own power. They were likely using the right words. But they had forgotten the power was not theirs, but God's. God's power is not accessed by ritual, but by faith. Actions or words without faith are powerless.

Jesus quickly did what his disciples could not do. The demon was no match for his power. The disciples were perplexed by the strength of this particular demon. They discovered that the problem was not the might of the demon but their lack of faith. Jesus was forced to remind them of that basic source of Christian strength—prayer.

This story sounds all too familiar, does it not? How often have we failed because of our reliance on own on strength? Do we pray in faith so that we might operate by the power of God? The world will continue to encounter a powerless church until we remember upon whose power we must depend.

"Dear God, help us clearly see our desperate need for faith in your power if we are to do your work. May we spend more time on our knees before you than working by our own strength."

TRUE GREATNESS?

(9:30-50)

DAY ONE READING AND QUESTIONS

³⁰They left that place and passed through Galilee. Jesus did not want anyone to know where they were, ³¹because he was teaching his disciples. He said to them, "The Son of Man is going to be betrayed into the hands of men. They will kill him, and after three days he will rise." ³²But they did not understand what he meant and were afraid to ask him about it.

1. Why did Jesus not want people to know where he was?

2. Why did Jesus keep repeating the message of his impending death?

3. Why do you think the disciples were afraid to ask Jesus what he meant?

DAY TWO READING AND QUESTIONS

³³They came to Capernaum. When he was in the house, he asked them, "What were you arguing about on the road?" ³⁴But they kept quiet because on the way they had argued about who was the greatest.

³⁵Sitting down, Jesus called the Twelve and said, "If anyone wants to be first, he must be the very last, and the servant of all."

³⁶He took a little child and had him stand among them. Taking him in his arms, he said to them, ³⁷"Whoever welcomes one of these

little children in my name welcomes me; and whoever welcomes me does not welcome me but the one who sent me."

1. Why were the disciples reluctant to reveal what they were discussing on the road?

2. Why were the disciples concerned about greatness?

3. What can we learn from Jesus' words regarding children?

DAY THREE READING AND QUESTIONS

[38]"Teacher," said John, "we saw a man driving out demons in your name and we told him to stop, because he was not one of us."

[39]"Do not stop him," Jesus said. "No one who does a miracle in my name can in the next moment say anything bad about me, [40]for whoever is not against us is for us. [41]tell you the truth, anyone who gives you a cup of water in my name because you belong to Christ will certainly not lose his reward.

1. What is ironic about this situation (remember the preceding encounter with a demon)?

2. What do we know about the man whose activity the disciples were trying to curtail?

3. What does it mean to "give a cup of water" in Jesus' name?

DAY FOUR READING AND QUESTIONS

[42]"And if anyone causes one of these little ones who believe in me to sin, it would be better for him to be thrown into the sea with a large millstone tied around his neck. [43]If your hand causes you to sin, cut it off. It is better for you to enter life maimed than with two hands to go into hell, where the fire never goes out. [45]And if your foot causes you

to sin, cut it off. It is better for you to enter life crippled than to have two feet and be thrown into hell. ⁴⁷And if your eye causes you to sin, pluck it out. It is better for you to enter the kingdom of God with one eye than to have two eyes and be thrown into hell, ⁴⁸where

> "'their worm does not die,
> and the fire is not quenched.'
⁴⁹Everyone will be salted with fire.

⁵⁰"Salt is good, but if it loses its saltiness, how can you make it salty again? Have salt in yourselves, and be at peace with each other."

1. Why is Jesus' warning here so pointed?

2. What do you think Jesus is saying about sin in this passage?

3. How does salt lose its saltiness? How do we have salt in ourselves?

DAY FIVE READING AND QUESTIONS

Reread the entire text (9:30-50).

1. Do you aspire for greatness? How so?

2. Do you take the time to love and encourage children? How might we do this with more intent?

3. How do you view sin? How do you view hell? How do you think we should live in view of this passage?

MEDITATION

Why do we yearn for greatness? Is this Satan's tug at our hearts? We are created in the image of God. Would that not cause us to seek greatness? The problem is not the seeking but how we define what we seek. Jesus came to teach us how to live a life of true significance to God's glory. Satan uses that God-given desire for greatness and distorts it so that it destroys us.

As Jesus' entourage journeyed towards Jerusalem, we should not be surprised that the disciples were concerned with who was the most important among them. They were convinced Jesus would be crowned Messiah. What positions of prominence would they hold in this new kingdom? It was their misunderstanding of the nature of God's kingdom that kept them from hearing what Jesus was teaching them about his imminent death.

Can you imagine how puzzled they must have been when Jesus told them that the prominence they sought could only be found by being a servant of all? He then took a child as an example of how to be close to Jesus. "Show attention to this child and you will be embracing me and the one who sent me." What could all this mean? It was radically different than anything they had considered.

The lesson for us in these episodes is clear: when we allow ourselves to think as the world thinks, we exclude ourselves from the activity and purposes of God. Are we more concerned about others who are not one of *our* group using the name of Jesus than faithfully living in his power and purpose? Do we ignore those Jesus would have us serve in order to serve those who benefit us? Do we disregard the danger of sin to satisfy the appetites of our bodies? Though it appears we are walking with Jesus and are proud to call ourselves Christian, if we are behaving like the disciples did in this reading, we are working against the kingdom.

Greatness. How will you pursue it? There is only one way to true greatness. Walk authentically with him who teaches us true greatness through serving those who have nothing to give in return.

"Lord, teach us to radiate your greatness through serving those whom others might not even see."

FAITHFUL?

(10:1-31)

DAY ONE READING AND QUESTIONS

¹⁰:¹Jesus then left that place and went into the region of Judea and across the Jordan. Again crowds of people came to him, and as was his custom, he taught them.

²Some Pharisees came and tested him by asking, "Is it lawful for a man to divorce his wife?"

³"What did Moses command you?" he replied.

⁴They said, "Moses permitted a man to write a certificate of divorce and send her away."

⁵"It was because your hearts were hard that Moses wrote you this law," Jesus replied. ⁶"But at the beginning of creation God 'made them male and female.' ⁷For this reason a man will leave his father and mother and be united to his wife, ⁸and the two will become one flesh.' So they are no longer two, but one. ⁹Therefore what God has joined together, let man not separate."

¹⁰When they were in the house again, the disciples asked Jesus about this. ¹¹He answered, "Anyone who divorces his wife and marries another woman commits adultery against her. ¹²And if she divorces her husband and marries another man, she commits adultery."

1. What do you think Jesus taught about when crowds gathered?

2. Why do you think the Pharisees asked Jesus about divorce?

3. Why did Jesus return to creation to answer the question concerning divorce?

DAY TWO READING AND QUESTIONS

[13]People were bringing little children to Jesus to have him touch them, but the disciples rebuked them. [14]When Jesus saw this, he was indignant. He said to them, "Let the little children come to me, and do not hinder them, for the kingdom of God belongs to such as these. [15]I tell you the truth, anyone who will not receive the kingdom of God like a little child will never enter it." [16]And he took the children in his arms, put his hands on them and blessed them.

1. Why do you think people brought little children to Jesus at a time when this would have been seen as disrespectful of an important person?

2. Why do you think the disciples attempted to turn the children away?

3. How does one receive the kingdom like a child?

DAY THREE READING AND QUESTIONS

[17]As Jesus started on his way, a man ran up to him and fell on his knees before him. "Good teacher," he asked, "what must I do to inherit eternal life?"

[18]"Why do you call me good?" Jesus answered. "No one is good— except God alone. [19]You know the commandments: 'Do not murder, do not commit adultery, do not steal, do not give false testimony, do not defraud, honor your father and mother.'"

[20]"Teacher," he declared, "all these I have kept since I was a boy."

[21]Jesus looked at him and loved him. "One thing you lack," he said. "Go, sell everything you have and give to the poor, and you will have treasure in heaven. Then come, follow me."

[22]At this the man's face fell. He went away sad, because he had great wealth.

[23]Jesus looked around and said to his disciples, "How hard it is for the rich to enter the kingdom of God!"

[24]The disciples were amazed at his words. But Jesus said again, "Children, how hard it is to enter the kingdom of God! [25] It is easier for a camel to go through the eye of a needle than for a rich man to enter the kingdom of God."

1. What do you think caused the man to fall on his knees before Jesus?

2. Why did Jesus ask the man to sell all he had and give it to the poor?

3. Why did Jesus say it was hard for the rich to enter the kingdom of heaven?

DAY FOUR READING AND QUESTIONS

[26]The disciples were even more amazed, and said to each other, "Who then can be saved?"

[27]Jesus looked at them and said, "With man this is impossible, but not with God; all things are possible with God."

[28]Peter said to him, "We have left everything to follow you!"

[29]"I tell you the truth," Jesus replied, "no one who has left home or brothers or sisters or mother or father or children or fields for me and the gospel [30]will fail to receive a hundred times as much in this present age (homes, brothers, sisters, mothers, children and fields—and with them, persecutions) and in the age to come, eternal life. [31]But many who are first will be last, and the last first."

1. Why were the disciples perplexed by Jesus' response to the rich man?

2. Why was Peter anxious to acknowledge what he had given up to follow Jesus?

3. What does Jesus mean by the first being last and the last being first?

DAY FIVE READING AND QUESTIONS

Reread the entire text (10:1-31).

1. What should we learn from the teachings of Jesus concerning divorce in our day?

2. How can we be the kind of person who parents want their children to be around? What does this tell us about Jesus?

3. What do you think Jesus might ask you to give up in order to follow him?

MEDITATION

The religious leaders were always putting Jesus to the test with their questions. But Jesus hardly ever answered the question. Oh, he responded, but not with a direct answer. Why didn't Jesus just say, "No, you can't divorce!"? In this case, there was a more important question, and that is what Jesus answered: "What does God intend to happen in marriage?" To get to his point, he answered the question with another question, "What did Moses command?" Jesus then turned them from Moses' concession to their hard hearts to the real question, "What does God intend to happen in marriage?" It is not just about avoiding divorce. It is about God forming two into one. It is God who conjoins us—his intent is that man and woman become one in marriage. No human being should consider separating what God has joined.

One of the most wonderful attributes of Jesus was his "approachability." Isn't it wonderful that people knew they could bring their little children to Jesus for a blessing? This was a culture where children were considered of little worth—yet Jesus wanted them brought to him. He even used them as an example of how to receive God's kingdom. When a child is given a gift, he or she receives it with great joy and no hesitation. An adult often forgets the joy of receiving gifts. Only when we understand the kingdom in such a way that we receive it with unreserved joy will we receive it at all.

In some cases, even the rich approached Jesus. I wonder why? Might they have seen in him an expression of joyful life for which they longed but could not find? Why else would the wealthy man fall on his knees and ask where life might be found? Eternal life for the Jew wasn't life after death, it was life in God's messianic kingdom. It was a life without end—for sure—but it was also life abiding in God's will here on earth. This young man was perplexed. He had it all, yet there was a longing from deep within for something greater. He saw in Jesus what he desperately wanted. Jesus' answer to the man's longing was shocking. It was similar to how Jesus responded to Nicodemus in John's gospel. "You won't find life in what you are currently accumulating. You have to start over. Sell what you don't need and give it to those who need it. Then I can show you the life you seek. Only when you give up on your life as it now stands will you be able to follow me."

So, what is keeping you and me from true life? In what do we trust rather than God? What do we pursue other than authentic righteousness? Whatever it might be, get rid of it. It isn't worth it. Whatever you have to give up in order to be a true disciple of Jesus, give it up. You will receive infinitely more from the giver of life.

"Lord, give me the courage to admit I have false gods. Teach me to turn away from them that I might find life in you."

TRUE GREATNESS II

(10:32-52)

DAY ONE READING AND QUESTIONS

³²They were on their way up to Jerusalem, with Jesus leading the way, and the disciples were astonished, while those who followed were afraid. Again he took the Twelve aside and told them what was going to happen to him. ³³"We are going up to Jerusalem," he said, "and the Son of Man will be betrayed to the chief priests and teachers of the law. They will condemn him to death and will hand him over to the Gentiles, ³⁴who will mock him and spit on him, flog him and kill him. Three days later he will rise."

1. At what were the disciples astonished? (see the previous story)

2. Why is Jesus again telling them of his death?

3. Why do you think the disciples—even after his death—did not anticipate his resurrection?

DAY TWO READING AND QUESTIONS

³⁵Then James and John, the sons of Zebedee, came to him. "Teacher," they said, "we want you to do for us whatever we ask." ³⁶"What do you want me to do for you?" he asked.

³⁷They replied, "Let one of us sit at your right and the other at your left in your glory."

³⁸"You don't know what you are asking," Jesus said. "Can you drink the cup I drink or be baptized with the baptism I am baptized with?"

³⁹"We can," they answered.

Jesus said to them, "You will drink the cup I drink and be baptized with the baptism I am baptized with, ⁴⁰but to sit at my right or left is not for me to grant. These places belong to those for whom they have been prepared."

1. *Why did James and John ask Jesus to say "yes" before they made their request?*

2. *What did James and John want from Jesus?*

3. *Of what baptism did Jesus speak? What do you think James and John thought he was asking?*

DAY THREE READING AND QUESTIONS

⁴¹When the ten heard about this, they became indignant with James and John. ⁴²Jesus called them together and said, "You know that those who are regarded as rulers of the Gentiles lord it over them, and their high officials exercise authority over them. ⁴³Not so with you. Instead, whoever wants to become great among you must be your servant, ⁴⁴and whoever wants to be first must be slave of all. ⁴⁵For even the Son of Man did not come to be served, but to serve, and to give his life as a ransom for many."

1. *Why were the ten indignant?*

2. *What does it mean to "lord over" or "exercise authority over?"*

3. *What did Jesus come to do and how should that influence how we see our lives?*

DAY FOUR READING AND QUESTIONS

[46]Then they came to Jericho. As Jesus and his disciples, together with a large crowd, were leaving the city, a blind man, Bartimaeus (that is, the Son of Timaeus), was sitting by the roadside begging. [47]When he heard that it was Jesus of Nazareth, he began to shout, "Jesus, Son of David, have mercy on me!"

[48]Many rebuked him and told him to be quiet, but he shouted all the more, "Son of David, have mercy on me!"

[49]Jesus stopped and said, "Call him."

So they called to the blind man, "Cheer up! On your feet! He's calling you." [50]Throwing his cloak aside, he jumped to his feet and came to Jesus.

[51]"What do you want me to do for you?" Jesus asked him.

The blind man said, "Rabbi, I want to see."

[52]"Go," said Jesus, "your faith has healed you." Immediately he received his sight and followed Jesus along the road.

1. *What is significant about what Bartimaeus called Jesus?*

2. *Why would the crowd rebuke a blind man crying for mercy?*

3. *Why did Jesus ask the blind man what he wanted?*

DAY FIVE READING AND QUESTIONS

Reread the entire text (10:32-10:52).

1. *Why is it important for us to know that Jesus knew exactly what was going to happen when he arrived in Jerusalem?*

2. *Do you embrace Jesus' call to be a servant? Why or why not?*

3. *Did you catch the irony of the blind man knowing Jesus as Messiah (Son of David)? Why could he see what others could not?*

MEDITATION

Jesus knew what was coming. His disciples thought they knew. Even though Jesus told them plainly he was about to die, his followers continued to posture themselves for the kingdom they expected. James and John requested what all the disciples wanted. The others were not indignant because the brothers' request was inappropriate; they were upset because James and John asked before the rest of them did. So Jesus took this opportunity to again attack the false view of greatness so evident among Jesus' followers. Gentiles (those who did not know any better) demonstrated their power through domination over others, but not disciples of Jesus.

We need to once again hear the voice of Jesus speaking to us—personally. Exercising authority over another is not a demonstration of divine power. It is a false substitute. Serving is a true manifestation of power. That is the essence of the incarnation—Jesus coming as the word of God made flesh. The Son of Man came to show us that life is found not only in serving, but in totally giving oneself for the benefit of others.

How would today's world regard those of us who follow Jesus if we truly embraced just this one teaching of Jesus? There would be no grasping for power among us; there would only be sacrificial love. We would be constantly available, not only for each other, but for all. Jesus came to establish a kingdom of servants, not lords.

In the midst of all the confusion about Jesus, there was one who saw Jesus for who he was. Ironically, the man was blind. When Bartimaeus heard Jesus was coming through on the way to Jerusalem, he knew it was his only chance. The crowd was embarrassed by his cry for Jesus' attention. In their thinking, important rabbis on their way to Jerusalem had no time for beggars. But Bartimaeus would not be silenced. No—for he was certain Messiah was near. He called out in desperation a prayer that continues to be said by countless followers of Jesus to this day, "Jesus, Son of David, have mercy on me." And, of course, Jesus did. Asked by Jesus what he wanted, he asked for sight. Consider the confusion in which the disciples were living. They weren't asking for sight. They were too busy anticipating the power they thought they were about to receive. They weren't asking for mercy. They thought they could see, but were blind.

Jesus is passing close by, right now. For what do we ask?

"Jesus, Son of David, have mercy on me."

THE TRUMPHAL ENTRY AND TEACHING AT THE TEMPLE

(11:1-33)

DAY ONE READING AND QUESTIONS

¹As they approached Jerusalem and came to Bethpage and Bethany at the Mount of Olives, Jesus sent two of his disciples, ²saying to them, "Go to the village ahead of you, and just as you enter it, you will find a colt tied there, which no one has ever ridden. Untie it and bring it here. ³If anyone asks you, 'Why are you doing this?' tell him, 'The Lord needs it and will send it back here shortly.' "

⁴They went and found a colt outside in the street, tied at a doorway. As they untied it, ⁵some people standing there asked, "What are you doing, untying that colt?" ⁶They answered as Jesus had told them to, and the people let them go. ⁷When they brought the colt to Jesus and threw their cloaks over it, he sat on it. ⁸Many people spread their cloaks on the road, while others spread branches they had cut in the fields. ⁹Those who went ahead and those who followed shouted,

"Hosanna!'"

"Blessed is he who comes in the name of the Lord!"

¹⁰"Blessed is the coming kingdom of our father David!"

"Hosanna in the highest!"

¹¹Jesus entered Jerusalem and went to the temple. He looked around at everything, but since it was already late, he went out to Bethany with the Twelve.

1. *Why is it important to understand that Jesus knew everything that was to happen, even the particulars?*

2. *Why do you think the people were so excited about Jesus' arrival in Jerusalem?*

3. *What do you think Jesus was thinking as he looked at the temple?*

DAY TWO READING AND QUESTIONS

[12]The next day as they were leaving Bethany, Jesus was hungry. [13]Seeing in the distance a fig tree in leaf, he went to find out if it had any fruit. When he reached it, he found nothing but leaves, because it was not the season for figs. [14]Then he said to the tree, "May no one ever eat fruit from you again." And his disciples heard him say it.

[15]On reaching Jerusalem, Jesus entered the temple area and began driving out those who were buying and selling there. He overturned the tables of the money changers and the benches of those selling doves, [16]and would not allow anyone to carry merchandise through the temple courts. [17]And as he taught them, he said, "Is it not written:
   "'My house will be called
      a house of prayer for all nations'?
   But you have made it 'a den of robbers.'"'

[18]The chief priests and the teachers of the law heard this and began looking for a way to kill him, for they feared him, because the whole crowd was amazed at his teaching.

[19]When evening came, they went out of the city.

1. *What is the connection between the fig tree and Jerusalem?*

2. *How had the temple become a den of robbers?*

3. *Why did the leaders want to kill Jesus?*

DAY THREE READING AND QUESTIONS

[20]In the morning, as they went along, they saw the fig tree withered from the roots. [21]Peter remembered and said to Jesus, "Rabbi, look! The fig tree you cursed has withered!"

[22]"Have faith in God," Jesus answered. [23]"I tell you the truth, if anyone says to this mountain, 'Go, throw yourself into the sea,' and does not doubt in his heart but believes that what he says will happen, it will be done for him. [24]Therefore I tell you, whatever you ask for in prayer, believe that you have received it, and it will be yours. [25]And when you stand praying, if you hold anything against anyone, forgive him, so that your Father in heaven may forgive you your sins.'"

1. What is significant about the fig tree being withered?

2. Why does Jesus answer Peter's question with a statement about faith?

3. What does Jesus say about faith?

DAY FOUR READING AND QUESTIONS

[27]They arrived again in Jerusalem, and while Jesus was walking in the temple courts, the chief priests, the teachers of the law and the elders came to him. [28]"By what authority are you doing these things?" they asked. "And who gave you authority to do this?"

[29]Jesus replied, "I will ask you one question. Answer me, and I will tell you by what authority I am doing these things. [30]John's baptism—was it from heaven, or from men? Tell me!"

[31]They discussed it among themselves and said, "If we say, 'From heaven,' he will ask, 'Then why didn't you believe him?' [32]But if we say, 'From men'...." (They feared the people, for everyone held that John really was a prophet.)

[33]So they answered Jesus, "We don't know."

Jesus said, "Neither will I tell you by what authority I am doing these things."

1. *Why were the elders questioning Jesus' authority?*

2. *Why did Jesus answer their question with a question of his own?*

3. *What does the response of the religious leaders show about the condition of their hearts?*

DAY FIVE READING AND QUESTIONS

Reread the entire text (11:1-33).

1. *What would Jesus see if he came to our places of worship?*

2. *How might we at times be like the barren fig tree—looking like a tree bearing fruit but having nothing to offer a starving world?*

3. *What can we learn from Jesus in the way he answered questions which were less than sincere?*

MEDITATION

The disciples must have been absolutely thrilled! Jesus was being accepted into Jerusalem just as they had anticipated—as one to be crowned king! Jesus went directly to the temple and "looked around at everything" and then returned to Bethany. Mark wants to make sure we see the connection between Jesus looking at the temple and the area surrounding it and the cursing of the fig tree. The tree was in full leaf, in stark contrast to the other trees. It was too early in the spring to be in leaf. A fig tree in leaf should be full of fruit (the Mediterranean fig tree produces figs as it produces leaves), but this tree was not. It was, in a sense, claiming to be something that it was not. Surely the cursing of the fig tree is a shadow of the destruction that awaited Jerusalem.

How about us? What do we bear through our lives that feeds a world starving for purpose and meaning? Are we like those of Jesus' day who loved to display their faith in God at the temple but did nothing for God with their lives? If Jesus came today and visited God's temple (our bodies), what would he find in the courts? What would Jesus clear out of our lives—what does not belong in God's temple? Has his house once again been reduced to a place of self-serving commerce?

Jesus calls us to live by faith. He calls us to recognize the amazing place we have been given in the kingdom of God. Why would we exchange the power of faith for a religious system that causes us to question God instead of glorify him? These stories should challenge us to the core of our being. Where do we stand? Would we find ourselves so intent on defending our doctrines that we would question Jesus' authority?

"Dear Lord, may I bear fruit to feed a hungry world as a proclamation of my faith in you."

WISE ANSWERS DEFEAT THE OPPOSITION

(12:1-34)

DAY ONE READING AND QUESTIONS

^{12:1}He then began to speak to them in parables: "A man planted a vineyard. He put a wall around it, dug a pit for the winepress and built a watchtower. Then he rented the vineyard to some farmers and went away on a journey. ²At harvest time he sent a servant to the tenants to collect from them some of the fruit of the vineyard. ³But they seized him, beat him and sent him away empty-handed. ⁴Then he sent another servant to them; they struck this man on the head and treated him shamefully. ⁵He sent still another, and that one they killed. He sent many others; some of them they beat, others they killed.

⁶"He had one left to send, a son, whom he loved. He sent him last of all, saying, 'They will respect my son.'

⁷"But the tenants said to one another, 'This is the heir. Come, let's kill him, and the inheritance will be ours.' ⁸So they took him and killed him, and threw him out of the vineyard.

⁹"What then will the owner of the vineyard do? He will come and kill those tenants and give the vineyard to others. ¹⁰Haven't you read this scripture:

" 'The stone the builders rejected
     has become the capstone ;

105

[11]the Lord has done this,

and it is marvelous in our eyes' ?"

[12]Then they looked for a way to arrest him because they knew he had spoken the parable against them. But they were afraid of the crowd; so they left him and went away.

1. How does this parable impact you?

2. What does this parable teach us about our lives?

3. Why did this parable infuriate the detractors of Jesus?

DAY TWO READING AND QUESTIONS

[13]Later they sent some of the Pharisees and Herodians to Jesus to catch him in his words. [14]They came to him and said, "Teacher, we know you are a man of integrity. You aren't swayed by men, because you pay no attention to who they are; but you teach the way of God in accordance with the truth. Is it right to pay taxes to Caesar or not? [15]Should we pay or shouldn't we?"

But Jesus knew their hypocrisy. "Why are you trying to trap me?" he asked. "Bring me a denarius and let me look at it." [16]They brought the coin, and he asked them, "Whose portrait is this? And whose inscription?"

"Caesar's," they replied.

[17]Then Jesus said to them, "Give to Caesar what is Caesar's and to God what is God's."

And they were amazed at him.

1. Why do Jesus' detractors acknowledge his integrity?

2. How do you think they expected Jesus to answer their question?

3. What rightfully belongs to God that we should give him?

DAY THREE READING AND QUESTIONS

[18]Then the Sadducees, who say there is no resurrection, came to him with a question. [19]"Teacher," they said, "Moses wrote for us that if a man's brother dies and leaves a wife but no children, the man must marry the widow and have children for his brother. [20]Now there were seven brothers. The first one married and died without leaving any children. [21]The second one married the widow, but he also died, leaving no child. It was the same with the third. [22]In fact, none of the seven left any children. Last of all, the woman died too. [23]At the resurrection whose wife will she be, since the seven were married to her?"

[24]Jesus replied, "Are you not in error because you do not know the Scriptures or the power of God? [25]When the dead rise, they will neither marry nor be given in marriage; they will be like the angels in heaven. [26]Now about the dead rising—have you not read in the book of Moses, in the account of the bush, how God said to him, 'I am the God of Abraham, the God of Isaac, and the God of Jacob'? [27]He is not the God of the dead, but of the living. You are badly mistaken!"

1. How do you think the Sadducees expected Jesus to answer their question?

2. Of what does Jesus accuse the Sadducees?

3. How does Jesus' answer to the Sadducees impact your thinking about life after death?

DAY FOUR READING AND QUESTIONS

[28]One of the teachers of the law came and heard them debating. Noticing that Jesus had given them a good answer, he asked him, "Of all the commandments, which is the most important?"

[29]"The most important one," answered Jesus, "is this: 'Hear, O Israel, the Lord our God, the Lord is one. [30]Love the Lord your God

with all your heart and with all your soul and with all your mind and with all your strength.' [31]The second is this: 'Love your neighbor as yourself.' There is no commandment greater than these."

[32]"Well said, teacher," the man replied. "You are right in saying that God is one and there is no other but him. [33]To love him with all your heart, with all your understanding and with all your strength, and to love your neighbor as yourself is more important than all burnt offerings and sacrifices."

[34]When Jesus saw that he had answered wisely, he said to him, "You are not far from the kingdom of God." And from then on no one dared ask him any more questions.

1. *What motivated the teacher of the law to ask Jesus about the most important commandment?*

2. *Why did Jesus also provide the second commandment with the first?*

3. *Why did no one dare ask him questions after this?*

DAY FIVE READING AND QUESTIONS

Reread the entire text (12:1-34).

1. *If you could ask Jesus any question, what would you ask? Why?*

2. *In our lives, how can we observe Jesus' teaching to "Give to Caesar what is Caesar's and to God what is God's?"*

3. *What can we do to show those around us that our lives are founded on the two great commandments?*

MEDITATION

Such wisdom! It is amazing to see how Jesus responded to those who were trying to trap him with trick questions. You know these questions were carefully crafted after hours of discussion. You can almost hear them saying, "There is no way he can answer this!" Place yourself in their shoes (sandals?). Listen to the question come out of your mouth, then be stunned by the wisdom of Jesus' response. Then feel the weight of Jesus' answer. His answers not only exposed the hypocrisy of the questioners, but they challenge all of us to contemplate our own lives and attitudes. What have we given to Caesar (systems of worldly power) that should only be given to God? In whom or what do we ultimately place our trust? The emphasis of Jesus' response is not paying taxes, but rather giving our total self to God. Money bears the images of humankind, but living human beings bear the image of God.

The Sadducees were very proud of themselves! They used Scripture to prove their point. They had a water tight argument to prove there was no resurrection. Their problem was two fold: they were ignorant of Scripture, and they had a limited understanding of the power of God. It is easy for us to wag our fingers at the arrogance and ignorance of the Sadducees, but it would be better for us to take a careful look at our own treatment of the word of God. Do we use it to prove our own doctrinal positions, or do we open our hearts to the living God so that he might mold and change us?

In the midst of groups trying to trap Jesus with their trick questions, a teacher of the law was impressed with his answers. So he took the opportunity to ask what was most important to him—"What is the greatest commandment?" Can you imagine what a different world it would be if we would just obey these commandments? What would our lives be like if they were only about loving God (thereby turning away from all other gods) and loving humankind?

"Almighty God, may we gladly surrender our lives to you in undivided loyalty and uncompromised love. May our love for you be seen in our love for all humankind."

WHOSE SON IS THE CHRIST AND THE BEGINNING OF THE END

(12:35-13:2)

DAY ONE READING AND QUESTIONS

[35]While Jesus was teaching in the temple courts, he asked, "How is it that the teachers of the law say that the Christ is the son of David? [36]David himself, speaking by the Holy Spirit, declared:

"'The Lord said to my Lord:

"Sit at my right hand

until I put your enemies

under your feet."' [37] David himself calls him 'Lord.' How then can he be his son?"

The large crowd listened to him with delight.

1. Why do you think Jesus asked this question?

2. What does this quotation from Psalms tell us about the Christ?

3. Why would such a question delight the crowd?

DAY TWO READING AND QUESTIONS

[38]As he taught, Jesus said, "Watch out for the teachers of the law. They like to walk around in flowing robes and be greeted in the

marketplaces, [39]and have the most important seats in the synagogues and the places of honor at banquets. [40]They devour widows' houses and for a show make lengthy prayers. Such men will be punished most severely."

1. *What had happened to the teachers of the law to make them so self-focused?*

2. *What primary sin is Jesus describing as he describes the teachers of the law?*

3. *Why will those who act in such a way receive severe punishment?*

DAY THREE READING AND QUESTIONS

[41]Jesus sat down opposite the place where the offerings were put and watched the crowd putting their money into the temple treasury. Many rich people threw in large amounts. [42]But a poor widow came and put in two very small copper coins, worth only a fraction of a penny.

[43]Calling his disciples to him, Jesus said, "I tell you the truth, this poor widow has put more into the treasury than all the others. [44]They all gave out of their wealth; but she, out of her poverty, put in everything—all she had to live on."

1. *What do you think drew Jesus to watch the offering at the temple?*

2. *Do you think others were watching as the rich poured in their offerings?*

3. *Who actually gave more, the widow or the rich?*

DAY FOUR READINGS AND QUESTIONS

[1]As he was leaving the temple, one of his disciples said to him, "Look, Teacher! What massive stones! What magnificent buildings!"

²"Do you see all these great buildings?" replied Jesus. "Not one stone here will be left on another; every one will be thrown down."

1. *Why were the disciples impressed with the temple?*

2. *What had the disciples failed to see in their amazement?*

3. *Of all the things humankind has built, what impresses you most? Compare its significance to the works of God.*

DAY FIVE READING AND QUESTIONS

Reread the entire text (12:35-13:2).

1. *If Jesus were to ask us a question that would expose our lack of under-standing of God's work, what do you think it would be?*

2. *How do we avoid the trap of practicing religion to be seen by others?*

3. *What is most important to you when receiving a gift: its monetary value or the value it represents from the giver?*

MEDITATION

Jesus used scripture to expose the lack of faith and understanding of the religious leaders. With his quotation from Psalm 110, he demonstrated that the Messiah they were anticipating was too limited in purpose and scope. Their Messiah could only be David's son. The true Messiah would also be David's Lord!

The crowds delighted in Jesus' candor. They loved his honesty and integrity. They understood his commitment to truth. There is so much for us to learn from Jesus. How should we confront those who oppose us? If we seek the wisdom provided by God through his Holy Spirit, attempts to discredit us can be great opportunities to expose wrongful thinking and advance the kingdom.

In stark contrast to Jesus, the religious leaders of his day demonstrated little integrity. They were too concerned with appearance and self-importance to be distracted by authenticity. They demonstrated the foolishness of seeking attention rather than seeking God. As a stunning indictment of the pompous behavior of the religious leaders and the attention drawn by the rich clanging their many coins into the temple treasury, an unseen widow approached and quietly gave her bread money to God. Jesus drew his disciples to him and again shocked them with his reaction to their desire for attention. "Look at the widow," he said. My guess is they thought, "The widow? What widow?" "The widow—the one who has the attention of God himself. The rest is just noise." She gave more. She gave in faith, choosing to believe that somehow God would provide for her needs.

What impresses us? What do we seek? Do we see what God sees? Do we hear what God hears? Are we moved by the work of humanity? If so, we are too easily impressed.

"Creator of all things, forgive us when we seek the approval of those around us rather than living to praise only you. Open our eyes to see what you see."

SIGNS OF THE END

(13:3-37)

DAY ONE READING AND QUESTIONS

³As Jesus was sitting on the Mount of Olives opposite the temple, Peter, James, John and Andrew asked him privately, ⁴"Tell us, when will these things happen? And what will be the sign that they are all about to be fulfilled?"

⁵Jesus said to them: "Watch out that no one deceives you. ⁶Many will come in my name, claiming, 'I am he,' and will deceive many. ⁷When you hear of wars and rumors of wars, do not be alarmed. Such things must happen, but the end is still to come. ⁸Nation will rise against nation, and kingdom against kingdom. There will be earthquakes in various places, and famines. These are the beginning of birth pains.

⁹"You must be on your guard. You will be handed over to the local councils and flogged in the synagogues. On account of me you will stand before governors and kings as witnesses to them. ¹⁰And the gospel must first be preached to all nations. ¹¹Whenever you are arrested and brought to trial, do not worry beforehand about what to say. Just say whatever is given you at the time, for it is not you speaking, but the Holy Spirit.

¹²"Brother will betray brother to death, and a father his child. Children will rebel against their parents and have them put to death.

¹³All men will hate you because of me, but he who stands firm to the end will be saved.

1. Why were Peter, James, and John concerned about when these things of which Jesus spoke would happen?

2. For what is Jesus preparing his disciples?

3. What is Jesus' fundamental message in these verses for his followers?

DAY TWO READING AND QUESTIONS

¹⁴"When you see 'the abomination that causes desolation' standing where it does not belong—let the reader understand—then let those who are in Judea flee to the mountains. ¹⁵Let no one on the roof of his house go down or enter the house to take anything out. ¹⁶Let no one in the field go back to get his cloak. ¹⁷How dreadful it will be in those days for pregnant women and nursing mothers! ¹⁸Pray that this will not take place in winter, ¹⁹because those will be days of distress unequaled from the beginning, when God created the world, until now—and never to be equaled again. ²⁰If the Lord had not cut short those days, no one would survive. But for the sake of the elect, whom he has chosen, he has shortened them. ²¹At that time if anyone says to you, 'Look, here is the Christ!' or, 'Look, there he is!' do not believe it. ²²For false Christs and false prophets will appear and perform signs and miracles to deceive the elect—if that were possible. ²³So be on your guard; I have told you everything ahead of time.

1. As Jesus describes the day Jerusalem will fall, how do you think the disciples heard these words?

2. Who are the false "Christs" of which Jesus forewarns?

3. What is the basic message of these verses?

DAY THREE READING AND QUESTIONS

²⁴ "But in those days, following that distress,

" 'the sun will be darkened,

and the moon will not give its light;

²⁵the stars will fall from the sky,

and the heavenly bodies will be shaken.'

²⁶"At that time men will see the Son of Man coming in clouds with great power and glory. ²⁷And he will send his angels and gather his elect from the four winds, from the ends of the earth to the ends of the heavens.

²⁸"Now learn this lesson from the fig tree: As soon as its twigs get tender and its leaves come out, you know that summer is near. ²⁹Even so, when you see these things happening, you know that it is near, right at the door. ³⁰I tell you the truth, this generation will certainly not pass away until all these things have happened. ³¹Heaven and earth will pass away, but my words will never pass away.

1. How do you envision the coming of "the Son of Man"?

2. What can we still learn from the fig tree?

3. What do we have from God that we know will never pass away? Do we live as if we know this is true?

DAY FOUR READING AND QUESTIONS

³²"No one knows about that day or hour, not even the angels in heaven, nor the Son, but only the Father. ³³Be on guard! Be alert! You do not know when that time will come. ³⁴It's like a man going away: He leaves his house and puts his servants in charge, each with his assigned task, and tells the one at the door to keep watch.

[35]"Therefore keep watch because you do not know when the owner of the house will come back—whether in the evening, or at midnight, or when the rooster crows, or at dawn. [36] If he comes suddenly, do not let him find you sleeping. [37]What I say to you, I say to everyone: 'Watch!' "

1. How will we know when Jesus will return?

2. What does it mean to live in such a way that we are "on guard" and "alert"?

3. How should we respond to Jesus' call to "Watch"?

DAY FIVE READING AND QUESTIONS

Reread the entire text (13:3-37).

1. This chapter is the most difficult to understand in Mark. What do you see as its main teaching?

2. What can we learn from this reading about the nature of history?

3. If the Lord returns in your lifetime, imagine what your response might be. Does anything in your life need to be changed?

MEDITATION

Much has been written concerning this chapter in Mark. Of what is Jesus speaking? Is it the destruction of Jerusalem or the end of time? Is it both? Where is the dividing line, if he is speaking of both?

There really is no certain answer to these questions. Review the possibilities provided by other commentaries. You will find there is no clear consensus. There does seem to be some specific instructions for helping the early Christians escape the destruction of Jerusalem. But exactly who the "abomination that causes desolation" might be is famously uncertain. However, the overarching message for all readers of these verses is clear: life in this world is uncertain. The future is not ours to count on or control. For certain, suffering and false prophets will come. There will be destructive wars and devastating events of nature. What are we to do about all this?

Meditate a few moments on each of the following statements: Live daily looking to the return of the Lord. Watch for deception. Do not be surprised when you are called to suffer. Observe the signs of nature that demonstrate that God is still in control of his world. Know that the Lord will surely return. Keep watch.

Jesus' final word in this reading is "Watch."

How do we live "watchfully"? This is a key expression of Christian hope. We intentionally live each day as if it is the day Jesus will return. We do not know when he will come. Only the Father knows. So Jesus is clearly not giving us predictive signs in this passage. Rather he wants us to be aware of his return so that the events of this world do not distract us from living for him, and him alone. He is coming! Watch!

"Lord, may we live with our eyes looking for your return. Every moment of the day may our hearts be fully invested in that which you would have us be."

THE LORD'S SUPPER

(14:1-31)

DAY ONE READING AND QUESTIONS

¹⁴:¹Now the Passover and the Feast of Unleavened Bread were only two days away, and the chief priests and the teachers of the law were looking for some sly way to arrest Jesus and kill him. ²"But not during the Feast," they said, "or the people may riot."

³While he was in Bethany, reclining at the table in the home of a man known as Simon the Leper, a woman came with an alabaster jar of very expensive perfume, made of pure nard. She broke the jar and poured the perfume on his head.

⁴Some of those present were saying indignantly to one another, "Why this waste of perfume? ⁵It could have been sold for more than a year's wages and the money given to the poor." And they rebuked her harshly.

⁶"Leave her alone," said Jesus. "Why are you bothering her? She has done a beautiful thing to me. ⁷The poor you will always have with you, and you can help them any time you want. But you will not always have me. ⁸She did what she could. She poured perfume on my body beforehand to prepare for my burial. ⁹I tell you the truth, wherever the gospel is preached throughout the world, what she has done will also be told, in memory of her."

1. What did the leaders fear as they plotted to kill Jesus?

2. When had they decided to kill him? What would change their plans?

3. What do Jesus' comments concerning the actions of the woman teach us about judgment of other's actions?

DAY TWO READING AND QUESTIONS

[10]Then Judas Iscariot, one of the Twelve, went to the chief priests to betray Jesus to them. [11]They were delighted to hear this and promised to give him money. So he watched for an opportunity to hand him over.

[12]On the first day of the Feast of Unleavened Bread, when it was customary to sacrifice the Passover lamb, Jesus' disciples asked him, "Where do you want us to go and make preparations for you to eat the Passover?"

[13]So he sent two of his disciples, telling them, "Go into the city, and a man carrying a jar of water will meet you. Follow him. [14]Say to the owner of the house he enters, 'The Teacher asks: Where is my guest room, where I may eat the Passover with my disciples?' [15]He will show you a large upper room, furnished and ready. Make preparations for us there."

[16]The disciples left, went into the city and found things just as Jesus had told them. So they prepared the Passover.

1. Why were the leaders delighted with Judas' offer?

2. Again we see that Jesus knew exactly what was to happen. Why is this important?

3. What do you think the disciples anticipated in this observation of Passover?

DAY THREE READING AND QUESTIONS

[17]When evening came, Jesus arrived with the Twelve. [18] While they were reclining at the table eating, he said, "I tell you the truth, one of you will betray me—one who is eating with me."

[19]They were saddened, and one by one they said to him, "Surely not I?"

[20]"It is one of the Twelve," he replied, "one who dips bread into the bowl with me. [21]The Son of Man will go just as it is written about him. But woe to that man who betrays the Son of Man! It would be better for him if he had not been born."

1. *How do you think Jesus' foretelling his betrayal first impacted the disciples? Imagine being at the table and hearing Jesus say this.*

2. *What does their response—"surely not I"—indicate? (Note: perhaps they were afraid of inadvertently betraying?)*

3. *Was Judas culpable, or was it the will of God for him to betray Jesus?*

DAY FOUR READING AND QUESTIONS

[22]While they were eating, Jesus took bread, gave thanks and broke it, and gave it to his disciples, saying, "Take it; this is my body."

[23]Then he took the cup, gave thanks and offered it to them, and they all drank from it.

[24]"This is my blood of the covenant, which is poured out for many," he said to them. [25]"I tell you the truth, I will not drink again of the fruit of the vine until that day when I drink it anew in the kingdom of God."

[26]When they had sung a hymn, they went out to the Mount of Olives.

[27]"You will all fall away," Jesus told them, "for it is written:

"'I will strike the shepherd,
> and the sheep will be scattered.'

[28]But after I have risen, I will go ahead of you into Galilee."

[29]Peter declared, "Even if all fall away, I will not."

[30]"I tell you the truth," Jesus answered, "today—yes, tonight—before the rooster crows twice you yourself will disown me three times."

[31]But Peter insisted emphatically, "Even if I have to die with you, I will never disown you." And all the others said the same.

1. What do you think the disciples understood Jesus was saying when he said, "This is my body," and "This is my blood of the covenant"?

2. What information does Jesus provide about his post-resurrection appearance?

3. Why do you think Peter was so confident that he would never fall away?

DAY FIVE READING AND QUESTIONS

Reread the entire text (14:1-31).

1. Have you ever received a lavish gift that was clearly a sacrifice for the one giving it? Reflect on how Jesus responded to the woman's gift of perfume.

2. Imagine being at the table with Jesus and his disciples at that last supper. Listen to the words of Jesus as he prepared his disciples for the coming events.

3. What can we learn from Peter's false sense of confidence?

MEDITATION

Consider the wide rage of emotions Jesus experienced in the events portrayed in these verses. The religious leaders wanted him killed, and he knew it. Sitting in the home of a cured leper, Jesus received a lavish gift of anointing with an expensive perfume. It was a wonderful demonstration of passionate devotion—a pure expression of thanksgiving to the Lord for what he had done in that person's life. As Jesus was enjoying the gift, those around him grumbled about the waste it represented. They even rebuked the giver harshly. Jesus reminded them to see the gift and what it symbolized. This woman was doing more than she even imagined—she was preparing him for burial. What a tender scene! And then, right at this point Judas betrayed Jesus to the religious leaders. "Oh, Lord, how do you put up with us?" I weep.

Then Jesus sat at the table we have come to love for what it provides. It is the Lord's table, an invitation to hear the story of redemption once again and renew our covenant relationship with God. But before the feast, there is the tragic news of betrayal. Joy and pain, love and indignant accusation, betrayal and commitment to follow no matter where the path leads. So it was in the life of Jesus. He endured it all, so that we might sit at the table with him. We are invited to the table even if we are weak, mistaken, confused, or maybe over-confident of our faithfulness. Even the betrayer was permitted to dip his bread and eat with Jesus.

We take the bread and remember the reality of Jesus in the flesh. We think of all the suffering—not just on the cross—but in all that Jesus did. He experienced it all so that we might hold the cup, the blood of the covenant, and rejoice that our sins are forgiven. The kingdom of God is ours as a gift.

What do you think about when you come to the Lord's table? There is no emotion, no pain, no experience that cannot be brought to the table. We come as we are and remember the story of God's redemptive love. We remember that Jesus came to experience the mess of humanity in order to give us new life. With great confidence we proclaim, "We will never leave you or disobey you!" only to find ourselves failing once again. Just the same, the invitation stands. Come to the table.

"Bread of life and healer of all wounds through your blood, may we truly give our lives to you. Help us remember you are the one who gave us life through your sacrifice, that we might willingly give our lives to you."

A GARDEN PRAYER AND BETRAYAL

(14:32-65)

DAY ONE READING AND QUESTIONS

³²They went to a place called Gethsemane, and Jesus said to his disciples, "Sit here while I pray." ³³He took Peter, James and John along with him, and he began to be deeply distressed and troubled. ³⁴"My soul is overwhelmed with sorrow to the point of death," he said to them. "Stay here and keep watch."

³⁵Going a little farther, he fell to the ground and prayed that if possible the hour might pass from him. ³⁶*"Abba*, Father," he said, "everything is possible for you. Take this cup from me. Yet not what I will, but what you will."

³⁷Then he returned to his disciples and found them sleeping. "Simon," he said to Peter, "are you asleep? Could you not keep watch for one hour? ³⁸Watch and pray so that you will not fall into temptation. The spirit is willing, but the body is weak."

³⁹Once more he went away and prayed the same thing. ⁴⁰When he came back, he again found them sleeping, because their eyes were heavy. They did not know what to say to him.

⁴¹Returning the third time, he said to them, "Are you still sleeping and resting? Enough! The hour has come. Look, the Son of Man is betrayed into the hands of sinners. ⁴²Rise! Let us go! Here comes my betrayer!"

1. How do you think the disciples reacted to Jesus' comments about his deep sorrow?

2. *What did Jesus want more than anything else?*

3. *Why were the disciples not able to sense the impending danger?*

DAY TWO READING AND QUESTIONS

[43]Just as he was speaking, Judas, one of the Twelve, appeared. With him was a crowd armed with swords and clubs, sent from the chief priests, the teachers of the law, and the elders.

[44]Now the betrayer had arranged a signal with them: "The one I kiss is the man; arrest him and lead him away under guard." [45]Going at once to Jesus, Judas said, "Rabbi!" and kissed him. [46]The men seized Jesus and arrested him. [47]Then one of those standing near drew his sword and struck the servant of the high priest, cutting off his ear.

[48]"Am I leading a rebellion," said Jesus, "that you have come out with swords and clubs to capture me? [49]Every day I was with you, teaching in the temple courts, and you did not arrest me. But the Scriptures must be fulfilled." [50]Then everyone deserted him and fled.

[51]A young man, wearing nothing but a linen garment, was following Jesus. When they seized him, [52]he fled naked, leaving his garment behind.

1. *What is ironic about the way Judas greeted Jesus?*

2. *Why did one of Jesus' disciples react violently to his arrest?*

3. *What was Jesus' point in his reaction to the crowd who arrested him?*

DAY THREE READING AND QUESTIONS

[53]They took Jesus to the high priest, and all the chief priests, elders and teachers of the law came together. [54]Peter followed him at a distance, right into the courtyard of the high priest. There he sat with the guards and warmed himself at the fire. [55]The chief priests and the whole

Sanhedrin were looking for evidence against Jesus so that they could put him to death, but they did not find any. [56]Many testified falsely against him, but their statements did not agree. [57]Then some stood up and gave this false testimony against him: [58]"We heard him say, 'I will destroy this man-made temple and in three days will build another, not made by man.'" [59]Yet even then their testimony did not agree.

1. Why was Peter following at a distance?

2. Why was it so difficult to find accord regarding the charge they should bring against Jesus?

3. Of what temple was Jesus speaking when he said it would be destroyed, yet rebuilt in three days?

DAY FOUR READING AND QUESTIONS

[60]Then the high priest stood up before them and asked Jesus, "Are you not going to answer? What is this testimony that these men are bringing against you?" [61]But Jesus remained silent and gave no answer.

Again the high priest asked him, "Are you the Christ, the Son of the Blessed One?"

[62]"I am," said Jesus. "And you will see the Son of Man sitting at the right hand of the Mighty One and coming on the clouds of heaven."

[63]The high priest tore his clothes. "Why do we need any more witnesses?" he asked. [64]"You have heard the blasphemy. What do you think?"

They all condemned him as worthy of death. [65]Then some began to spit at him; they blindfolded him, struck him with their fists, and said, "Prophesy!" And the guards took him and beat him.

1. Why did Jesus remain silent at the first period of his "trial"?

2. Why did Jesus answer the high priest when asked if he was the Christ, the Son of God?

3. Why was Jesus accused of blasphemy? Why is this ironic?

DAY FIVE READING AND QUESTIONS

Reread the entire text (12:32-65).

1. Have you experienced a Gethsemane moment in your walk with God? (not my will, but yours be done?) Reflect on that moment.

2. What do you think you would have done if you were one of the twelve with Jesus at the moment of his arrest?

3. What can we learn from Jesus about when to be silent and when to respond?

MEDITATION

These events in the life of Jesus are almost too painful to consider. Disciples too tired to show concern regarding Jesus' agony, even though he made it plain that he was in deep sorrow. A pleading before God not to suffer separation from him (the "cup"), yet Jesus' willingness to do whatever was necessary to obey his Father. The sounds of the approaching mob. "Teacher." Then a kiss of betrayal from a friend. In that moment, Jesus must have felt utterly abandoned and alone. And he was. Yet he did not waver. What strength! What love! What commitment to God's will!

What a shocking turn of events! I can't help but wonder what the disciples were thinking as they ran for their lives while the Lord was tied up and led away. Peter dared to follow at a distance. I wonder where we would be? Would we be Judas? Surely not! Would we be one of the many who fled? Would we lash out with our sword? Would we follow at a safe distance? Or would we be in the arresting mob? Would we be among the religious leaders trying desperately to find a way to accuse Jesus of a crime for which we could have him eliminated? Would we be Jesus? In all the confusion, in all the chaos, lying, and fear, there was only one who was at peace. Only one knew who he was and where he was going. Only one was not afraid.

Where do we choose to live? If we follow Jesus to the garden and submit our lives fully to the only one who deserves our trust, we follow Jesus to joy and peace. We free ourselves of the constant posturing demanded by our world. There would be no place for fear. Ironic, isn't it? In the events leading to the death of Jesus, he continued to show us how to live. The phrase, "Nevertheless, not my will, but yours be done," is the key to a life free from anxiety. It may mean we are falsely accused. It may mean we are mistreated. But we will never be abandoned. Even if the pain is so intense we cry out, "My God, why have you forsaken me?" Whatever happens to a faithful believer, God will use to advance his purposes. No fear. Not when you are committed to abiding in the will of God.

"Loving Abba Father, we ask that the cup of suffering be lifted from us. Nevertheless, not our will, but yours be done."

A PAINFUL DENIAL AND A SHAMEFUL TRIAL

(14:66–15:24)

DAY ONE READING AND QUESTIONS

⁶⁶While Peter was below in the courtyard, one of the servant girls of the high priest came by. ⁶⁷When she saw Peter warming himself, she looked closely at him.

"You also were with that Nazarene, Jesus," she said.

⁶⁸But he denied it. "I don't know or understand what you're talking about," he said, and went out into the entryway.

⁶⁹When the servant girl saw him there, she said again to those standing around, "This fellow is one of them." ⁷⁰Again he denied it.

After a little while, those standing near said to Peter, "Surely you are one of them, for you are a Galilean."

⁷¹He began to call down curses on himself, and he swore to them, "I don't know this man you're talking about."

⁷²Immediately the rooster crowed the second time. Then Peter remembered the word Jesus had spoken to him: "Before the rooster crows twice you will disown me three times." And he broke down and wept.

1. What do you think Peter experienced when he was first identified as a follower of Jesus?

2. Peter was likely identified as a Galilean by his speech. What do you think he was talking about to those around him?

3. How do you think Peter felt at the moment of realizing what he had done?

DAY TWO READING AND QUESTIONS

[1]Very early in the morning, the chief priests, with the elders, the teachers of the law and the whole Sanhedrin, reached a decision. They bound Jesus, led him away and handed him over to Pilate.

[2]"Are you the king of the Jews?" asked Pilate.

"Yes, it is as you say," Jesus replied.

[3]The chief priests accused him of many things. [4]So again Pilate asked him, "Aren't you going to answer? See how many things they are accusing you of."

[5]But Jesus still made no reply, and Pilate was amazed.

1. What had the Jewish leaders decided to do with Jesus?

2. Why do you think Jesus answered Pilate's question about being king?

3. Why, then, did Jesus not respond to the accusations make by the chief priests?

DAY THREE READING AND QUESTIONS

[6]Now it was the custom at the Feast to release a prisoner whom the people requested. [7]A man called Barabbas was in prison with the insurrectionists who had committed murder in the uprising. [8]The crowd came up and asked Pilate to do for them what he usually did.

[9]"Do you want me to release to you the king of the Jews?" asked Pilate, [10]knowing it was out of envy that the chief priests had handed Jesus over to him. [11]But the chief priests stirred up the crowd to have Pilate release Barabbas instead.

[12]"What shall I do, then, with the one you call the king of the Jews?" Pilate asked them.

[13]"Crucify him!" they shouted.

[14]"Why? What crime has he committed?" asked Pilate.

But they shouted all the louder, "Crucify him!"

[15]Wanting to satisfy the crowd, Pilate released Barabbas to them. He had Jesus flogged, and handed him over to be crucified.

1. How did Pilate know the chief priests brought Jesus to him out of envy?

2. Do you think Pilate really thought the Jews would ask for Jesus' release?

3. What was Pilate's ultimate motivation for allowing Jesus to be crucified?

DAY FOUR READING AND QUESTIONS

[16]The soldiers led Jesus away into the palace (that is, the Praetorium) and called together the whole company of soldiers. [17]They put a purple robe on him, then twisted together a crown of thorns and set it on him. [18]And they began to call out to him, "Hail, king of the Jews!" [19]Again and again they struck him on the head with a staff and spit on him. Falling on their knees, they paid homage to him. [20]And when they had mocked him, they took off the purple robe and put his own clothes on him. Then they led him out to crucify him.

[21]A certain man from Cyrene, Simon, the father of Alexander and Rufus, was passing by on his way in from the country, and they forced him to carry the cross. [22]They brought Jesus to the place called Golgotha (which means The Place of the Skull). [23]Then they offered him wine mixed with myrrh, but he did not take it. [24]And they crucified him. Dividing up his clothes, they cast lots to see what each would get.

1. What comes to your mind when you think of the "crown of thorns"?

2. Why did the soldiers mock Jesus? What did they have to gain from this?

3. Why did Jesus not accept pain-killing wine mixed with myrrh?

DAY FIVE READING AND QUESTIONS

Reread the entire text (14:66-15:24).

1. *Do these events influence in any way your day-to-day life? How or why not?*

2. *What does the example of Jesus teach us about how we should respond to unfair or undeserved punishment?*

3. *After reading of all the miracles performed by Jesus, the reader has to believe that Jesus could have stopped the proceedings at any moment. Why did he submit to such treatment and pain?*

MEDITATION

It is beyond our ability to grasp the ends to which Jesus was willing to go to redeem us. This reading was intentionally organized to begin with Peter's denial. It reminds us that it was in the context of miserable human weakness that Jesus was willing to die. All of his suffering, all of the shame, the mocking, the absurdity of the Son of God being subjected to such treatment—all of this for us, weak and undeserving as we are. How should we respond to such love?

Can you imagine the deep pain Jesus must have felt knowing that, as he was suffering mistreatment at the hands of the religious leaders, Peter, out of fear, was denying he even knew Jesus? Think of how it must have shattered Jesus' heart to hear the crowds who once hailed him as king cry, "Crucify him!" How could he allow those Roman soldiers to do what they did to him? The flogging, the crown of thorns, the cross. It is too much. Perhaps Mark uses few words to describe what Jesus suffered to keep from breaking us under the burden of guilt. But the message is clear: Jesus, the Son of God, came not to be served, but to serve and give his life as a ransom for many.

Again, the question arises, "Where am I in the story?" Let me speak for myself. In a sense, I am in all the wrong places. I am the religious leader trying to protect my comfortable life. I am Peter, denying I know him in critical moments. I am Pilate, with the power to stand for what is right, but succumbing to the pressure of the expectation of others. I am the soldier, benefitting from someone else's needless suffering. I am the crowd shouting, "Crucify him!" And how could it be that Barabbas was released? A murderer, an insurrectionist. He deserved death, not freedom! Ah, here I am again—I am Barabbas, perhaps most of all; I who deserve death, am granted freedom. How can I do anything other than beg for forgiveness and submit my life to God's Holy Spirit? Of all the characters from this crucial moment in history, I need to be Jesus. He is the one character in the story I am not. But God is faithful....

"Dear God, please change me from within. I am mindful of how unworthy I am of your love. May I use the gift of redemption to become the image of Jesus to those around me."

THE SON OF GOD CRUCIFIED
(15:25-47)

DAY ONE READING AND QUESTIONS

[25]It was the third hour when they crucified him. [26]The written notice of the charge against him read: THE KING OF THE JEWS. [27]They crucified two robbers with him, one on his right and one on his left. [29]Those who passed by hurled insults at him, shaking their heads and saying, "So! You who are going to destroy the temple and build it in three days, [30]come down from the cross and save yourself!"

[31]In the same way the chief priests and the teachers of the law mocked him among themselves. "He saved others," they said, "but he can't save himself! [32]Let this Christ, this King of Israel, come down now from the cross, that we may see and believe." Those crucified with him also heaped insults on him.

1. *On the placard that normally identified the charge against the one crucified, what was written instead?*

2. *What is ironic about those who were challenging Jesus to fulfill what he said about destroying and rebuilding the temple?*

3. *Why didn't Jesus descend from the cross in order to prove who he was?*

DAY TWO READING AND QUESTIONS

[33]At the sixth hour darkness came over the whole land until the ninth hour. [34]And at the ninth hour Jesus cried out in a loud voice,

"Eloi, Eloi, lama sabachthani?"—which means, "My God, my God, why have you forsaken me?"

³⁵When some of those standing near heard this, they said, "Listen, he's calling Elijah."

³⁶One man ran, filled a sponge with wine vinegar, put it on a stick, and offered it to Jesus to drink. "Now leave him alone. Let's see if Elijah comes to take him down," he said.

³⁷With a loud cry, Jesus breathed his last.

1. What is your reaction to Jesus' cry of intense pain from the cross?

2. Why did some think Jesus was calling Elijah?

3. Do you think some actually thought Elijah might come down? Why do you think Mark included this detail?

DAY THREE READING AND QUESTIONS

³⁸The curtain of the temple was torn in two from top to bottom. ³⁹And when the centurion, who stood there in front of Jesus, heard his cry and saw how he died, he said, "Surely this man was the Son of God!"

⁴⁰Some women were watching from a distance. Among them were Mary Magdalene, Mary the mother of James the younger and of Joses, and Salome. ⁴¹In Galilee these women had followed him and cared for his needs. Many other women who had come up with him to Jerusalem were also there.

1. Why did Mark tell of the curtain of the temple and then offer no explanation?

2. Why are the words of the centurion central to the message of Mark?

3. Why does Mark mention the women who were present?

DAY FOUR READING AND QUESTIONS

⁴²It was Preparation Day (that is, the day before the Sabbath). So as evening approached, ⁴³Joseph of Arimathea, a prominent member of the Council, who was himself waiting for the kingdom of God, went boldly to Pilate and asked for Jesus' body. ⁴⁴Pilate was surprised to hear that he was already dead. Summoning the centurion, he asked him if Jesus had already died. ⁴⁵When he learned from the centurion that it was so, he gave the body to Joseph. ⁴⁶So Joseph bought some linen cloth, took down the body, wrapped it in the linen, and placed it in a tomb cut out of rock. Then he rolled a stone against the entrance of the tomb. ⁴⁷Mary Magdalene and Mary the mother of Joses saw where he was laid.

1. *What do we know of Joseph of Arimathea?*

2. *Why was Pilate surprised at the news of Jesus' death?*

3. *Why was so little done with Jesus' body before he was placed in the tomb?*

DAY FIVE READING AND QUESTIONS

Reread the entire text (15:25- 47).

1. *How does Mark's telling of the crucifixion compare to the other gospel accounts?*

2. *What emotion did you experience when you reread this text?*

3. *If you were hearing the story of Jesus for the first time, what would you be thinking?*

MEDITATION

Surely this is the most sacred text in Christian scripture. It was a moment so tragic the sun refused to shine. Crucifixion is one of the cruelest ways humanity has ever devised to cause a slow and painful death. A humiliating death. The charge against the condemned was nailed to the cross as a stark warning for anyone involved in wrongful behavior. "King of the Jews"—what kind of charge was that? Other gospel accounts tell us it was Pilate's way of vindicating Jesus to some extent. Mark gives us no explanation. In Mark's account, it seems to point to the failure of the Jews to establish any real charges against Jesus.

What tragic, yet joyful (for those of us who believe) irony! Those passing taunted Jesus, telling him that he couldn't even save himself, so how was he going to destroy and rebuild the temple in three days? If they had waited until Sunday to ask, they would have had the answer! Temple destroyed? With a broken heart we say, "Yes, he was crucified!" Restored in three days? YES!

Even deeper irony is found in those who challenged Jesus to prove he was the Christ by coming down from the cross. Had he done what they taunted, he would have demonstrated he was *not* the Christ. The Scriptures made it plain that the Christ was to suffer, die, and rise again. Jesus himself had said this repeatedly. The drastic deed must be done. And it was. Mark quickly summarized all of the agony of Jesus' sacrifice by recording the painful cry of Jesus: "My God, my God, why have you forsaken me?" Much has been written concerning this cry. Mark uses it to contrast the deep pain of Jesus with the unbelievably shallow curiosity of those witnessing his death. "What did he say? I think he is calling Elijah! Let's see if Elijah comes! This might be really interesting!" But Jesus, weak from the multiple beatings he had suffered, cried out loudly, and died.

Think about Jesus' cry of agony for a moment. Was he forsaken by God? Theologians continue to argue the exact meaning of the cry from Psalm 22. Here's what we can know. Jesus suffered beyond our ability to comprehend out of his love for the Father and for us. No greater pain can be imagined that Jesus being separated from his Father. Pause for a moment of quiet contemplation. "Oh, Lord, we are so thankful for your love for us."

The temple curtain was torn. Mark did not explain it. He left it for the reader to understand. In the theological climax of Mark's gospel, a Gentile centurion exclaimed what the Jewish leaders refused to see: "Surely this man was the Son of God." Why was this so hard for others to see? Whenever we find someone in Mark's gospel seeking healing, seeking help, or just observing without bias, they clearly see. Jesus is the Son of God.

Women who followed Jesus watched from a distance. Joseph of Arimathea, with great bravery, asked for the body of a condemned man. He wrapped the body of our Lord in a simple linen cloth and gently placed it in a grave. A stone was rolled over the tomb. It was nearly Sabbath, so no more could be done.

Do not move on to the resurrection. Not yet. Stop and consider what Mark has described in these 22 verses. Nine hours had passed, maybe less. Jesus was faithful to the end. For three hours that day darkness enveloped the sun. This was no eclipse. It seemed that evil had prevailed. The ultimate price had been paid. Satan had tried to tempt Jesus throughout his ministry. He offered power. He offered the world. Now Jesus had paid the price for being the faithful Son of God.

"Dear Jesus, the Christ, the Son of the living God, as we think of your lifeless, scarred body in the tomb, we remember what you were willing to do to remain faithful to your Father. Forgive us when we are so easily led astray. May we reflect often on your amazing example of submission to the will of God."

RESURRECTION!

(16:1-16)

DAY ONE READING AND QUESTIONS

¹⁶:¹When the Sabbath was over, Mary Magdalene, Mary the mother of James, and Salome bought spices so that they might go to anoint Jesus' body. ²Very early on the first day of the week, just after sunrise, they were on their way to the tomb ³and they asked each other, "Who will roll the stone away from the entrance of the tomb?"

⁴But when they looked up, they saw that the stone, which was very large, had been rolled away. ⁵As they entered the tomb, they saw a young man dressed in a white robe sitting on the right side, and they were alarmed.

1. *Why did the women wait until the first day of the week to anoint Jesus' body?*

2. *What was their concern on the way to the tomb?*

3. *What did they experience once they entered the tomb?*

DAY TWO READING AND QUESTIONS

⁶"Don't be alarmed," he said. "You are looking for Jesus the Nazarene, who was crucified. He has risen! He is not here. See the place where they laid him. ⁷But go, tell his disciples and Peter, 'He is going ahead of you into Galilee. There you will see him, just as he told you.' "

[8]Trembling and bewildered, the women went out and fled from the tomb. They said nothing to anyone, because they were afraid.

1. What three words reflect the greatest moment in human history?

2. Where were they to see Jesus?

3. Why were they bewildered and afraid after hearing the news of Jesus?

DAY THREE READING AND QUESTIONS

[The most reliable early manuscripts and other ancient witnesses do not include verses 9-20]

[9]When Jesus rose early on the first day of the week, he appeared first to Mary Magdalene, out of whom he had driven seven demons. [10]She went and told those who had been with him and who were mourning and weeping. [11]When they heard that Jesus was alive and that she had seen him, they did not believe it.

[12]Afterward Jesus appeared in a different form to two of them while they were walking in the country. [13]These returned and reported it to the rest; but they did not believe them either.

1. Why were the disciples so difficult to convince concerning the resurrection?

2. What do you think the disciples discussed in the time after the crucifixion before they saw the risen Lord?

3. Consider how difficult it would be for you to believe that someone dear to you had risen from the dead.

DAY FOUR READING AND QUESTIONS

[14]Later Jesus appeared to the Eleven as they were eating; he rebuked them for their lack of faith and their stubborn refusal to believe those who had seen him after he had risen.

[15]He said to them, "Go into all the world and preach the good news to all creation. [16]Whoever believes and is baptized will be saved, but whoever does not believe will be condemned. [17]And these signs will accompany those who believe: In my name they will drive out demons; they will speak in new tongues; [18]they will pick up snakes with their hands; and when they drink deadly poison, it will not hurt them at all; they will place their hands on sick people, and they will get well."

[19]After the Lord Jesus had spoken to them, he was taken up into heaven and he sat at the right hand of God. [20]Then the disciples went out and preached everywhere, and the Lord worked with them and confirmed his word by the signs that accompanied it.

1. *What message were the disciples to take to the world?*

2. *Do you feel compelled to share the news of the risen Lord? Why or why not?*

3. *One of the greatest evidences of the resurrection is the lives of the disciples. Something caused these distraught men and women to go everywhere proclaiming the message of the risen Lord. How are we to continue this witness?*

DAY FIVE READING AND QUESTIONS

Reread the entire text (16:1-16).

1. *Imagine walking up to the open tomb. How do you think you would have reacted when you saw that the tomb was opened?*

2. *If you read just through verse 8, can there be any doubt concerning the resurrection?*

3. *If Mark ended his text at verse 8, what might he be challenging his readers to consider?*

MEDITATION

Resurrection! "He is risen!" Three words that changed the world. Jesus, the faithful Son of God, had risen from the dead. All that Jesus said and did was vindicated in that moment. Now we reflect back over the teachings of Jesus and we hear his words, "The Son of Man must suffer many things, and be killed, and after three days rise again." He said it repeatedly. He said it openly and plainly. But his followers could not hear him. They couldn't even imagine it. Even when told by a heavenly messenger what had happened, the women could not believe it. They left the tomb bewildered and afraid.

Amazing, isn't it? All throughout the ministry of Jesus he clearly commanded those who witnessed his miracles not to tell anyone. Now, in the greatest moment in history, his followers are told to go and tell others of the resurrection, and they are bewildered and afraid. Surely the story does not end here!

What do we do with the ending of Mark's gospel? Long ending or short? The language changes with verse 9. It is for this reason that many believe the original gospel ended here. Verses 9-20 seem to be written in a very different style. Mark often used summary paragraphs throughout his gospel, but this final summary is significantly different in vocabulary and structure. Is it possible the original ending was lost? I suppose. But consider Mark's message. He begins by telling us this is the story of Jesus Christ, the Son of God. Repeatedly the text verifies his identity. He healed the sick, gave sight to the blind, cleansed the leper, calmed the storms, walked on water, cast our demons, fed the multitude, and even raised the dead. Further, time after time he told of his impending death and resurrection. At his death, the temple curtain was torn, the sun refused to shine, the centurion understood. This was indeed the Son of God.

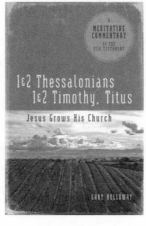

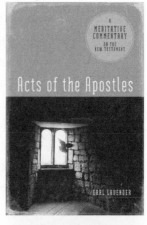
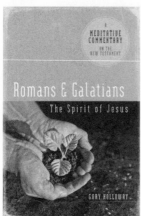
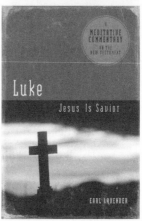